SANTA FE

Then and Now

SANTA FE

Then and Now

Sheila Morand

with photographs by
John Swenson

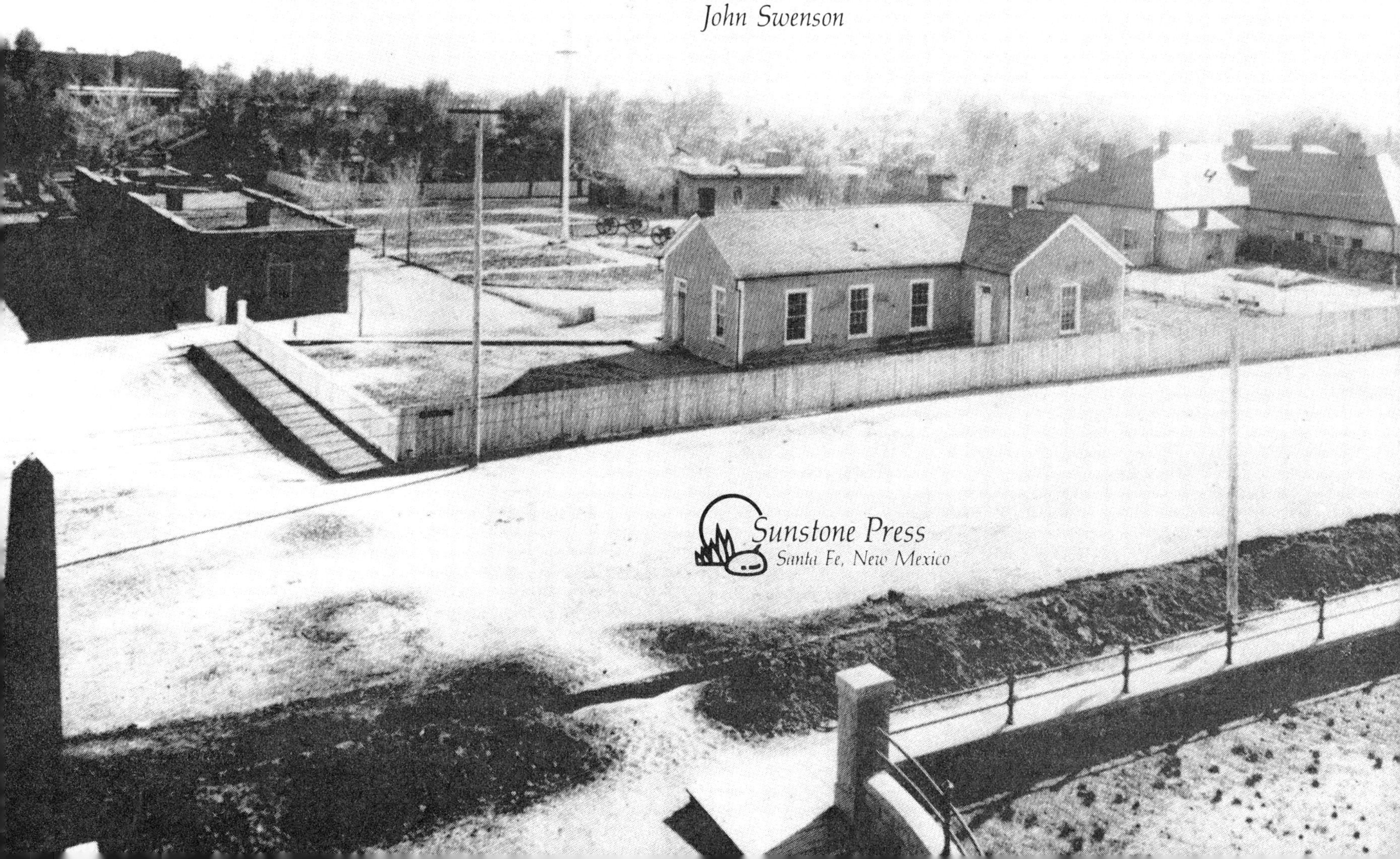

Sunstone Press
Santa Fe, New Mexico

To my husband, Jim Morand,
and friend, Carol Olwell,
both of whom
gave steady encouragement
and practical help.

REVISED EDITION
Printed in the United States of America

Library of Congress Cataloging in Publication Data:

Morand, Sheila, 1943–
Santa Fe then and now.

Bibliography; p.92.
Includes index.
1. Santa Fe (N.M.)—Buildings. 2. Historic buildings—New Mexico—Santa Fe. 3. Architecture—New Mexico—Santa Fe. 4. Santa Fe (N.M.)—Description. I. Title
F804. S28A26 1984 978.9'56 84—2503
ISBN: 0-86534-046-3

Originally Published in 1984 by Sunstone Press / Post Office Box 2321 / Santa Fe, NM 87504-2321 / USA

Table of Contents

Acknowledgments for the First Edition

I am especially grateful to J. Lathrop Viemeister whose support of, and belief in this project was gratifying and immediate. John Swenson, who made all the new photographs, was a pleasure to work with and did a beautiful job. Richard Rudisill and Arthur Olivas of the Museum of New Mexico photo archives and Orlando Romero of the New Mexico State Library were always encouraging and immensely helpful. Kathleen Brooker and Boyd Pratt of the Historic Preservation Bureau and Linda Tigges of the City Planning Office were gracious in providing maps and information. The New Mexico State Records Center and Archives staff were friendly and efficient in meeting my requests. Many others gave time, ideas or direction to my research for which I am most appreciative. My very special thanks go to Lila DeWindt, Dr. and Mrs. C. Gregory Crampton and Mary Jean Cook for the special information they supplied.

Foreword to the First Edition

Through its long history, spanning almost 400 years, Santa Fe has faced difficult challenges that have threatened its character and at times its very existence. It survived the factional strife between civil and religious officials of the 17th century, the Pueblo Revolt of 1680 (despite a 13-year period of exile for the Spaniards), and the economic isolation and defensive struggles of the 18th and early 19th centuries. With the independence of Mexico from Spain in 1821 came the opening of legal trade with the United States, and a stream of French and Anglo-American merchants into town via the Santa Fe Trail. The transfer of sovereignty from Mexico to the United States following the 1846 invasion of U.S. troops stimulated a greater influx of Easterners into Santa Fe, facilitated later in the century by the arrival of the railroad.

All of these historical developments have left their imprint on the physical appearance of Santa Fe. The design and scale of the buildings, the materials used in construction, the layout of the streets, all reflect the changing needs and cultural values of the inhabitants through the years. Yet despite the extreme demographic and cultural changes that have impacted Santa Fe, the character, pace and scale -- the *ambiente* -- of the town remained relatively undisturbed until recently. The "discovery" of Santa Fe by the outside world in the 1970s and 80s has resulted in drastic changes in the architecture and the very character of the town. Whether the community decides to accept these changes or to fight to preserve the character of Santa Fe remains yet to be determined.

This volume presents the opportunity to examine the ways in which the architecture of Santa Fe has changed over the years, as well as to see how certain elements have remained very much the same. Through this unique window into the past, we can observe the historical evolution of the community, and place the current architectural developments and controversies into a valuable historical context.

Stanley M. Hordes

Introduction to the First Edition

What did Santa Fe look like a hundred years ago? This book provides some insight into that question. It is meant for the new visitor to Santa Fe. The brief history accompanying the photographs is of necessity incomplete in many respects. Should the reader want to enrich his knowledge of Santa Fe and New Mexico with further reading, a bibliography is included.

Many important locations had to be left out of this publication. Unfortunately, not all of today's interesting sites were photographed a hundred years ago, either because the structure was already in disrepair or had disappeared from the scene by the time photographers came to the area or because the location was not important to that era. Vice versa, many of the wonderful sites photographed 80 to 100 years ago are difficult or impossible to re-photograph today because of trees or surrounding buildings. Others, tragically, have been turned into parking lots! A few sites were eliminated as simply uninteresting.

Without those intrepid and admirable early photographers, this book would have been impossible. Out of the abundant old photos available, I have included most of the well-known locations, a few lesser-known locations and a few that are little-known to the general public, i.e., have not appeared in publication before. Maps have been included so the reader can walk or drive to all locations and make his own comparison. Doing this really gives one a feeling of old Santa Fe, its antiquity and ambience.

I have divided the general map on page 9 into five sections: The Plaza (circled on the map and shown in an enlarged inset with the code "P"); Northeast (shown in more detail on page 27 and coded "NE"); Southeast (shown in detail on page 41 and coded "SE"); Southwest (shown in detail on page 65 and coded "SW"); and Northwest (shown in detail on page 79 and coded "NW.") By using the general map on page 9, you can take a tour of the locations shown in this book. Each location is coded for easy reference.

SANTA FE

Palace of the Governors
P2
Palace Ave.
Lincoln Ave.
Washington Ave.
P1
PLAZA
P3 The Guarantee
P4 Kiva Shop
P8
San Francisco St.
P5
P7
P6 La Fonda

NE7
Bishops Lodge Rd.
Artist Rd.
Paseo de la Cuma
NW7
Rosario Blvd.
Old Taos Hyway
Paseo de Peralta
Sunset
NE1
NW6
Federal Place
NE6
Paseo de Peralta
NE5
Griffin St.
NW4
Marcy St.
Lincoln Ave.
Washington Ave.
NW1
Grant Ave.
NW5
NW3
NW2
P2
NE2
NE3
Rodriguez
NE4
La Vereda
Palace Ave.
Palace Ave.
Plaza
SW7
P8
P1
P3
P4
SE3
Cathedral Place
SW1
SW6 San Francisco St.
P5
SE1
SE2
P7
P6
Water St.
SE4
SE5
Guadalupe
Sandoval
Galisteo
Don Gaspar
Shelby St.
Alameda
Alameda
Santa Fe River
Santa Fe River
Delgado
Camino Escondido
SE10
SE9
SE7
SW5
Agua Fria
Analco De Vargas St.
SW2
SE6
SE8
Old Santa Fe Trail
Paseo de Peralta
Acequia Madre
Camino del Monte Sol
SE11
Galisteo
SW4
Don Gaspar
Manhattan
Paseo de Peralta
SE12
El Caminito
Cerrillos Rd.
E. Coronado
SW3

THEN — THE PLAZA, ca. 1885

When Santa Fe was settled ca. 1610, the Plaza was laid out, with several deviations, according to the City Planning Ordinances of the Laws of the Indies issued by Philip II, King of Spain, in 1573. The plaza was the region's first religious, governmental and commercial center and is the best-documented place in New Mexico. It originally extended to the east as far as St. Francis Cathedral today, forming a rectangle. In Spanish colonial times the *plaza mayor*, as it was called, was dirt, a place for cockfights, fiestas, religious processions and daily markets. It was part of El Camino Real, sole trade route from Mexico City and the state of Chihuahua. To the north stood the Palace of the Governors, seat of government for 200 years before American traders arrived. To the east and later to the south stood parish churches, symbol of the Spanish mandate for the exploration and Christianization of the New World. Scattered in between were homes and gardens.

In 1821 Mexico became independent from Spain. The Plaza was renamed the Plaza of the Constitution. It became the terminus for a second trade route beginning 850 miles to the east in Independence, Missouri -- the famous Santa Fe Trail. The appearance of the Plaza began to change, reflecting the attitudes and values of the incoming Anglos, as all people neither Hispanic nor Indian are called. By 1846, when United States annexation took place, the Plaza had become a concentrated commercial center where supplies and trade goods were loaded, unloaded and distributed. A growing population of influential Easterners gradually turned the Plaza into a city park and, by 1863, the covered wagons, animal pens and picket lines of burros and mules had moved beyond the city center.

Architecture surrounding the Plaza had taken on the appearance of eastern cities. One-story

adobes were replaced by two-story frame buildings with shops and offices inside. A bandstand for the Fort Marcy band was built in the center of the Plaza in 1866 and by the 1880s it was defined by a white picket fence and benches. The fence originally had gates but they were frequently left open. Turnstiles were installed which proved effective in keeping out wandering horses.

NOW — THE PLAZA

Today, the Plaza is still the city center. For the younger generation it provides a place "to be seen"; for the older generation it's a pleasant place to which one can retreat for a few moments of quiet contemplation or to share the events of the day.

At the center of the Plaza stands the war monument, completed in 1868. It's dedicated to Union soldiers who fought in the Civil War and Indian wars. The Palace of the Governors remains to the north. The three business blocks surrounding the Plaza have been remodeled into Spanish-Pueblo Revival style architecture or simply painted an adobe color in order to blend with one another. In 1968, continuous portals (covered porches) were added to their façades to unify them.

In 1962 the Plaza was declared a National Historic Landmark. The Plaza, the Palace of the Governors and Santa Fe itself attract visitors from all over the world. In a world hastening toward franchised similarity, it continues to be The City Different.

THEN — PALACE OF THE GOVERNORS, ca. 1868 (inset ca. 1881)

The Palace of the Governors was originally constructed between 1610-1612 under the first governor of Santa Fe, Don Pedro de Peralta. It has undergone continuous renovation and repair since that time. The reason was its adobe construction. Adobe is a fragile building material subject to weathering. Without a protective outer surface, it gradually disintegrates into mud, whether it is adobe bricks such as the Spanish introduced or "puddled" walls (successive hand-formed layers) such as the Pueblo Indians built.

The Palace was never a palace. The very name is a misnomer. It is only one of many contradictions throughout New Mexico's history. It was called "Casa Real" or Royal House because it was the seat of government and the governor's residence. In the 1600s and 1700s it was part of the Spanish Presidio, which included several other buildings and cultivated fields. It was originally larger than it is today, having a chapel on the east end and dungeons on the west end. Descriptions given in early manuscripts indicated the doors were small and low and there were few windows. The roof was made of peeled logs (vigas) placed side by side with a layer of brush and hard-packed earth on top. Until 1877, when a tin roof was added, the Palace roof always leaked in a rainstorm. The only solution, one visitor noted, was to use an umbrella when inside! The floors

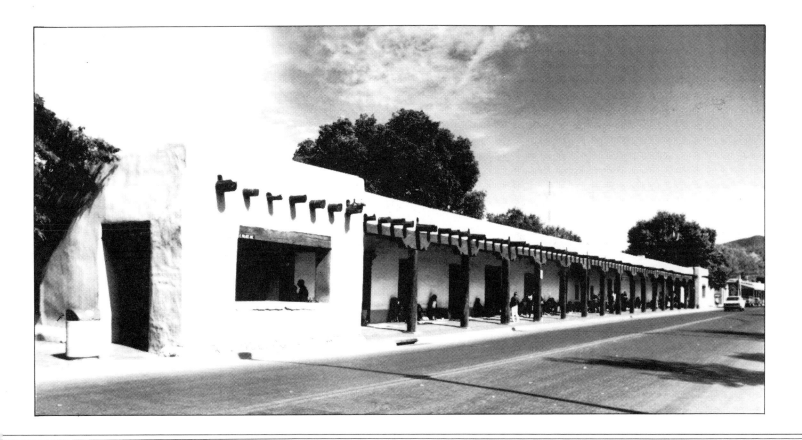

were hard-packed dirt, often mixed with ox blood to make a smooth surface. Photos taken in the 1850s show the façade was Spanish Colonial style with round hand-hewn columns along the portal.

The 1868 photo shows the portal with square, milled columns, having been modified by the U.S. Army into what became known as Territorial style architecture. The west end had been demolished two years earlier to make way for Lincoln Avenue. The telegraph had just arrived in Santa Fe -- the reason for the tall pole. New Mexico was a territory of the United States. From the Plaza trade routes went east to Independence, Missouri, along the Santa Fe Trail, or west to California via the California Trail.

NOW — PALACE OF THE GOVERNORS

A Victorian balustrade atop the portal completed the remodeling of the west end of the Palace in 1877. It made the rest of it look so shabby that the other tenants soon followed suit, each tenant being responsible for his own renovation. Glass windows had been installed and a plank sidewalk in front gave the Palace an air of respectability by 1881. By then it was the only single-story building on the Plaza.

The last government function was held in the Palace in 1907. In 1909 it became the Museum of New Mexico. From 1909 to 1913, it was remodeled into its present appearance by Jesse Nusbaum, archaeologist, photographer and first staff member of the Museum.

From 1610 to 1907 the Palace served as official headquarters under four governments: the Kingdom of Spain (1610-1821), the Empire of New Mexico (1821-1822), the Republic of Mexico (1823-1846), and the U.S. Territory of New Mexico (1846-1912).

Recent archaeological digs inside the Palace have revealed doors, walls, foundations and artifacts, some of which date back to the 1680s, the time of the Pueblo Revolt. The Palace continues to be one of the most fascinating building sites in America and the oldest government building still in use.

THEN — JOHNSON/CATRON BLOCK
ca. 1912 (inset ca. 1880)

In 1863 James L. Johnson, a merchant from Maryland, bought and improved buildings on the east side of the Plaza which became known as the Johnson block. By 1875 the *New Mexican*, Santa Fe's daily newspaper, described the newly renovated buildings in some detail. Johnson operated a drygoods store. At the time of the (top) picture, the corner building contained the

post office on the main floor and the Santa Fe Finishing School above. Johnson went bankrupt in 1881 and the block came into new ownership.

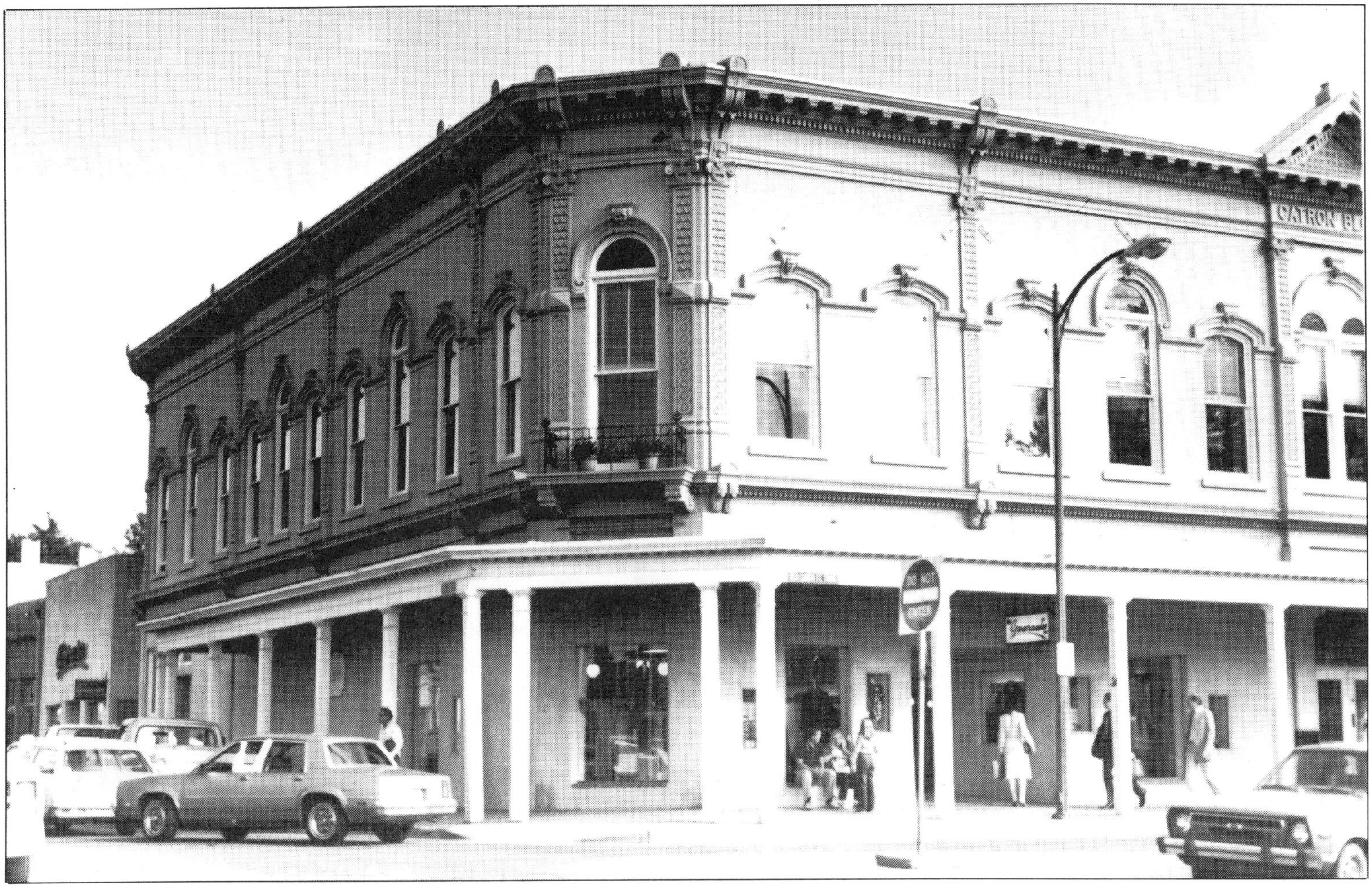

Thomas B. Catron acquired the property and by 1891 completed new brick buildings. Use followed that of the previous buildings with shops on the first floor and offices above. Catron was U.S. attorney, mayor of Santa Fe, U.S. Senator and a member of the Santa Fe Ring, a group of politicians, attorneys, businessmen and ranchers who dominated political and economic life in New Mexico in territorial days.

The White House opened in 1912, owned by Johanna Uhlfelder Blatt and her husband, Morris Blatt. It was Santa Fe's first fashion department store.

NOW

In a move toward uniformity, the brick building has been painted an adobe color and a portal added to blend with the Spanish-Pueblo Revival architecture of surrounding buildings.

THEN — FIRST NATIONAL BANK, 1913

Greek Revival architecture had been popular for institutions in the Midwest in the 1870s and 80s. First National Bank chose this style for their second bank building in 1912. New Mexico had just achieved statehood that year as the 47th state.

With the Palace of the Governors restoration underway in Spanish-Pueblo Revival style, the City Planning Board began earnest discussions regarding the preservation of historical buildings in the city. Numerous architectural styles were evident in the city by 1913 including Territorial, Italiante-Bracketed, Mansard and Queen Anne. Which should be preserved? Which prohibited?

P4

NOW

The City of Santa Fe eventually decided to allow only Spanish-Pueblo and Territorial style buildings in the city center. The bank was the last non-Pueblo style building constructed on the Plaza.

In 1957 the building was remodeled by the Santa Fe firm of Meem, Zehner, Holien & Associates in the Spanish-Pueblo Revival style. John Gaw Meem was one of New Mexico's leading architects and an enthusiast of what is today called the "Santa Fe style."

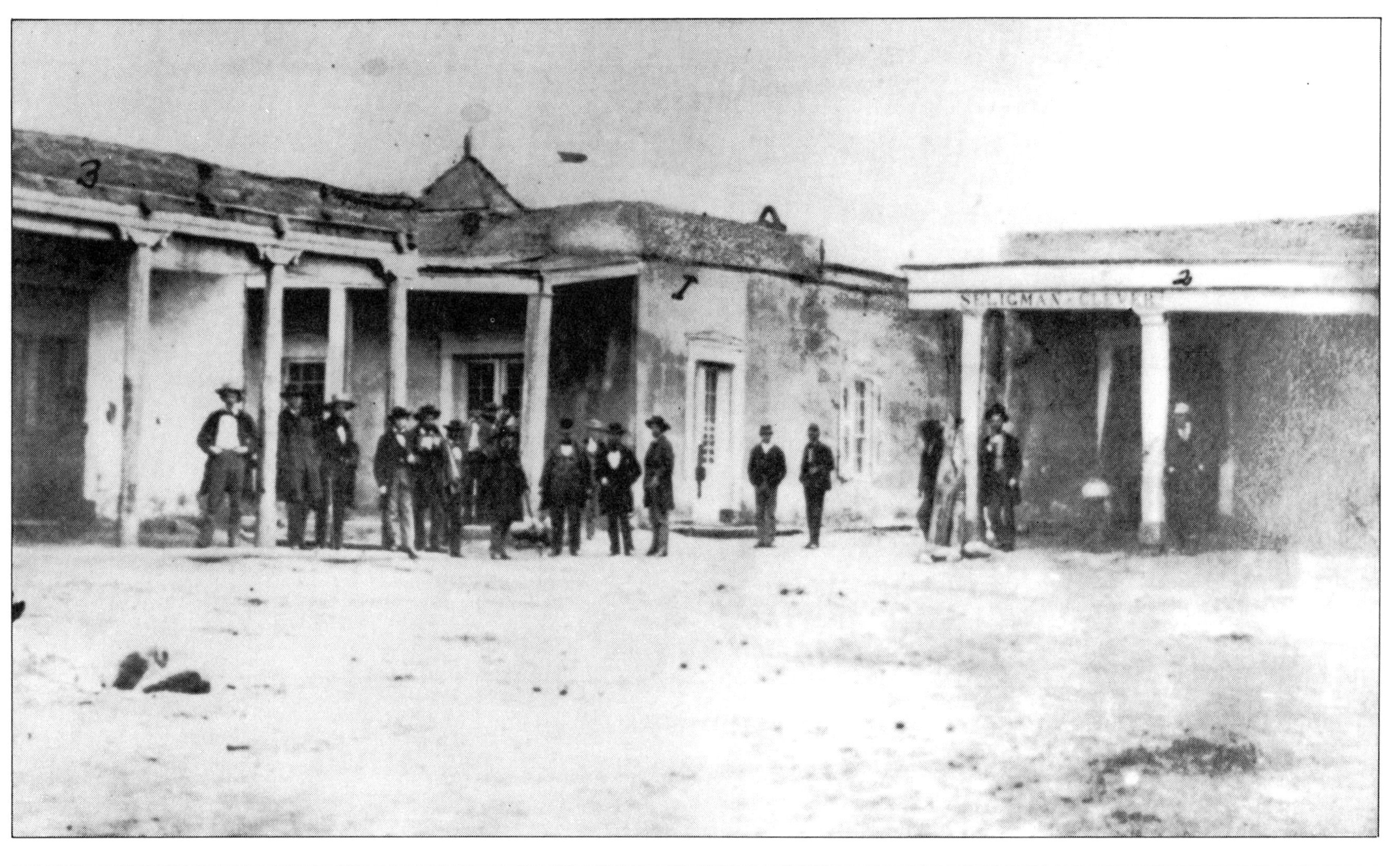

THEN — EXCHANGE HOTEL, ca. 1855-56

This is the earliest-known photograph of the southeast corner of the Plaza. The photographer is unknown. Foreshortening causes the buildings to appear much closer together than they actually were.

A *fonda* or inn was located on this corner prior to the opening of the Santa Fe Trail in 1822 but the name of it has been lost. At the time of this photo, the inn was called the Exchange Hotel. It was the only one in Santa Fe.

Seligman and Cleaver's store was established in 1855. Sigmund Seligman was one of New Mexico's early photographers and Charles P. Cleaver was a federal marshal and a territorial delegate to Congress. Their general mercantile store sold such items as liquor, groceries, cigars,

P5

clothing and carpets.

The building on the left is noted as a private residence on the photograph itself. Because of the round columns and zapata corbels (paired decorative timbers supporting the horizontal beams), typical of Spanish Colonial portals, its construction was probably pre-1846.

New Mexico had been a U.S. territory about 10 years at the time of this photo. Trade with the East had been established 30 years before but Santa Fe was still a remote and isolated city with a population of about 5,000.

NOW — LA FONDA HOTEL

The Exchange Hotel remained on the corner until 1919 when it was demolished. La Fonda was built two years later. Nothing remains of the earlier buildings to each side of the hotel. Each has had a series of occupants and face-lifts over the years. Undoubtedly, change will continue and the hundreds of stores that have done business beside the Plaza will continue to grow.

THEN — LA FONDA, ca. 1930
(inset ca. 1930)

The La Fonda Hotel, as photographed by T. Harmon Parkhurst around 1930, was still the end of the trail for Santa Fe visitors. It was constructed in 1921 at a cost of $200,000 by selling $50 shares to the public. The Spanish-Pueblo Revival design was the work of Rapp, Rapp & Hendrickson, a local firm.

In 1926 the Fred Harvey Company purchased the hotel from the local owners and, in 1929, enlarged it under the direction of John Gaw Meem. La Fonda was last remodeled in 1950 with a five-story rear addition.

Santa Fe's first tourists arrived by rail beginning in 1880. By the 1930s the city was well established as a tourist attraction. The Santa Fe Ticket Office, just north of La Fonda, arranged sightseeing tours to the nearby Indian pueblos in a 15-passenger touring car. These tours were called "Indian Detours."

NOW — LA FONDA HOTEL

La Fonda hosts small conventions, private parties and other social functions today as in years gone by. Its lovely interior is a fine example of one of the early large Spanish-Pueblo Revival designs. Its downtown location and first-rate facilities make it one of the finest old hotels in the U.S. As the oldest hotel site in America, La Fonda is continuing a long tradition in welcoming the latest arrivals to Santa Fe.

THEN — SAN FRANCISCO STREET
ca. 1889

U.S. occupation brought, in the words of Jenkins and Schroeder, *A Brief History of New Mexico,* "a virtual commercial revolution" to New Mexico from 1846 through 1900. Economic stability was attained through the presence of the U.S. Army, the end of Indian warfare and the coming of the railroad, which phased out covered wagon trade on the Santa Fe and California Trails. Much foreign capital came into New Mexico during the 1880s and merchants were established in fixed locations in the city. The Plaza was steadily evolving into the city's commercial center.

Jacob Solomon Spiegelberg, the first German immigrant to establish a business in Santa Fe, arrived with General Kearny's supply train in 1846. He was later joined by his four brothers. The first Spiegelberg store was built in 1881 on San Francisco Street. A year later they built a second building next to it. As the railroad had just arrived, the brothers were able to purchase metal cornices, English tiles, skylights and other building materials not available before.

Further down the block had been the location of the Spanish military chapel, La Castrense, built in 1790. By 1846 it was dilapidated and no longer in use. The incoming U.S. Army repaired it and maintained it as an arms store-

P7

house. In 1851 it was refitted as the U.S. District Court. Consternation among the Catholic population against the use of a church site for secular purposes, together with the arrival of Bishop Lamy in Santa Fe, resulted in the restoration of the church in 1853. But the location proved unsuitable for a church, so the property was sold to Simon Delgado in 1859 and a commercial enterprise was established there.

NOW — SAN FRANCISCO STREET

Both Spiegelberg buildings line San Francisco Street today, having been remodeled in the 1950s and 60s into Spanish-Pueblo Revival and Territorial style.

The influx of newcomers during the last half of the 19th century disrupted the religious unity long established among the Spanish colonists and Pueblo Indians. Today Santa Fe is a blend of four cultures (Spanish, Mexican, Indian and Anglo) whose differing religions, customs and values have enhanced each other economically and artistically. The economy is based largely on state government (the single largest employer), the arts (as evidenced by more than 100 galleries in the city) and tourism.

THEN — LINCOLN AVENUE
ca. 1865-66 (inset, ca. 1886-88)

One of the first two-story buildings to be built on the Plaza was the Perea & Company building shown above right. The Elsberg & Amberg building, next door, owned by two Santa Fe Trail traders, was more elaborate in design and housed their drygoods store. Bricks were not being made locally at this time. As a result,

P8

most new buildings were frame because the cost of importing brick over the Santa Fe Trail was prohibitive.

The corner of Lincoln and Palace has had many occupants over the years. By 1886 it was the Capital Hotel (inset); in the 1870s it was Z. Staab & Co., a general merchandise store; and by 1900 the offices of the *New Mexican* were located there.

NOW — LINCOLN AVENUE

The evolution of new businesses and new merchandise for sale has been continuous. In the 1920s this corner was known as the Cassell Building and housed a movie theater (starring such favorites as William Boyd and Mary Astor). In 1953-54 the Cassell Building was remodeled into the First National Bank (their third location on the Plaza). The present building, designed by architect John Gaw Meem, shows the decorum and classic formality which have been achieved in the evolution of the Spanish-Pueblo Revival style.

Dedication of the Cross of the Martyrs, Santa Fe Fiesta, September 1920

NORTHEAST

NE1

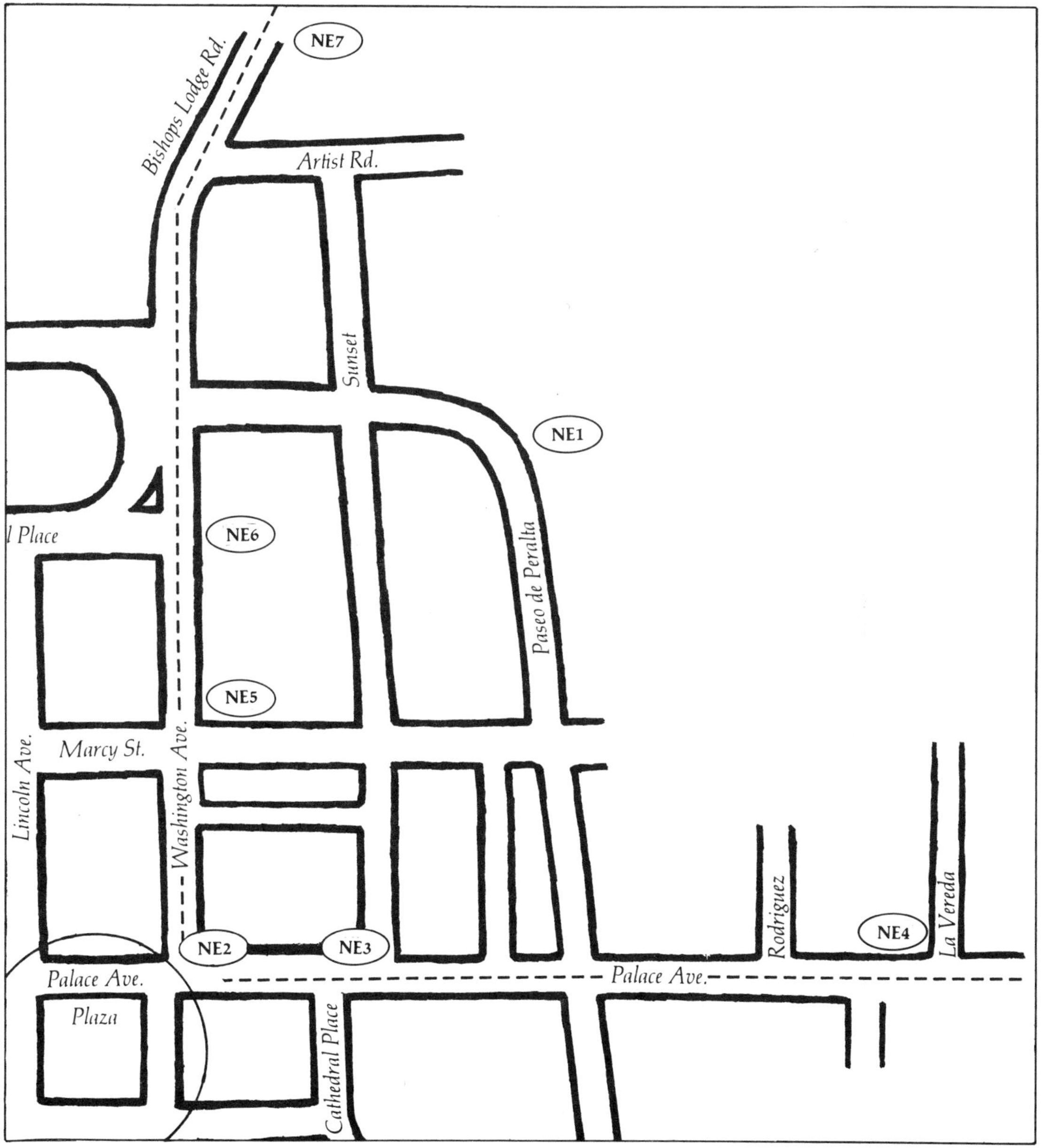

NE7
Bishops Lodge Rd.
Artist Rd.
Sunset
NE1
l Place
NE6
Paseo de Peralta
NE5
Marcy St.
Lincoln Ave.
Washington Ave.
Rodriguez
NE4
La Vereda
NE2
NE3
Palace Ave.
Palace Ave.
Plaza
Cathedral Place

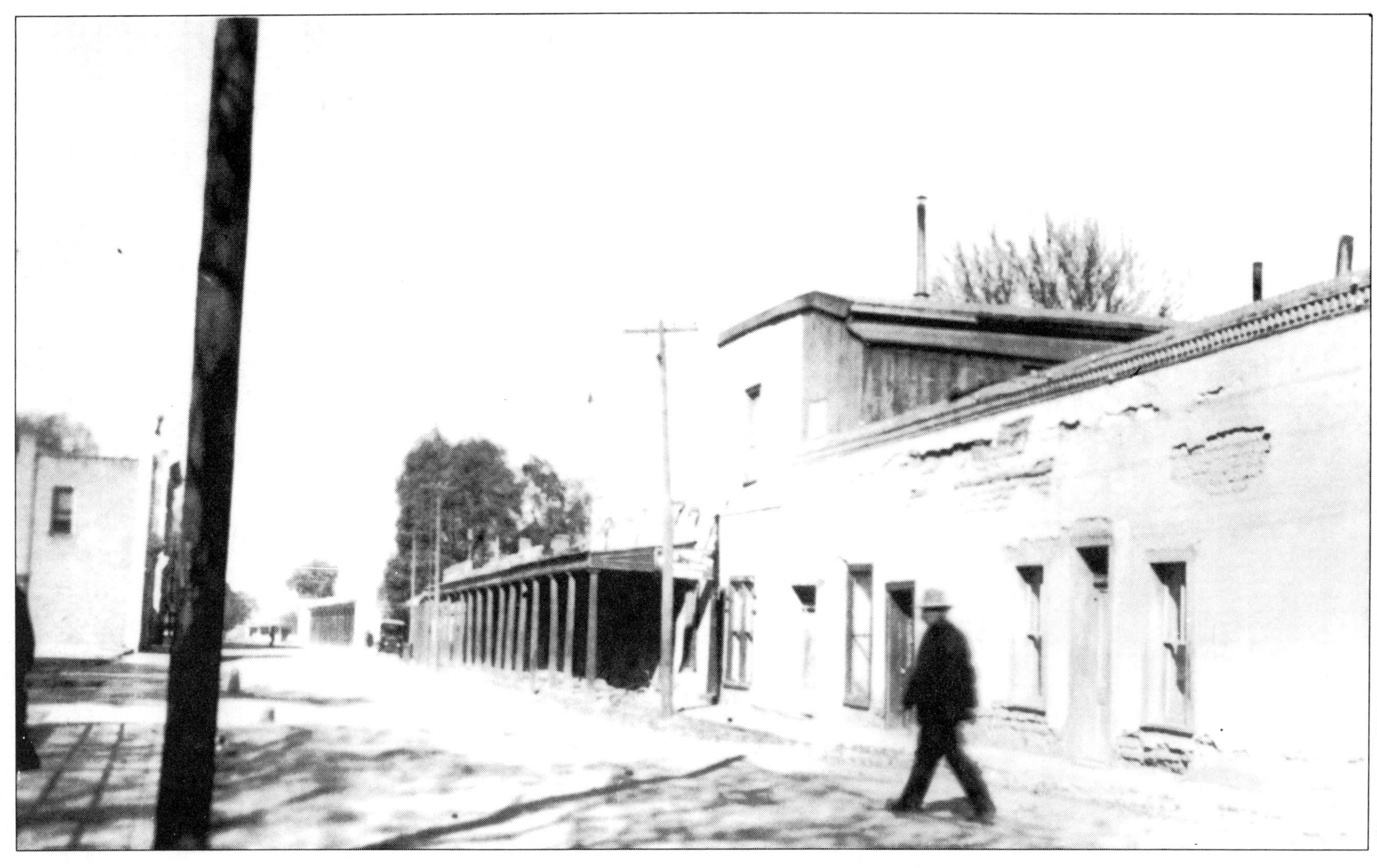

THEN — PRINCE & SENA PLAZA, ca. 1910-15

Historical records show the acreage was granted to Don Diego Arias de Quiros in 1698 by Governor General Diego de Vargas, the re-conqueror of Santa Fe after the Pueblo Revolt in 1680. The property changed owners many times in a fascinating series including important Spanish military personnel, Antoine Roubidoux (a famous French-Canadian trader), a governor and Supreme Court Justice (L. Bradford Prince) and a major in the Civil War (Jose D. Sena).

L. Bradford Prince purchased the western half of the property from Carmen de Benavides de Roubidoux in 1879, and he and his family made this their home for over 40 years. Major José D. Sena inherited the eastern half of the property and began construction of a large house in 1831. He and his wife had a total of 23 children and the hacienda eventually contained 33 rooms. Living quarters were on the south and west sides of the courtyard; the north side contained a coach house, storerooms and servants' quarters.

NE2

NOW — PRINCE & SENA PLAZA

Prince and Sena Plaza remain some of the finest examples of Spanish Colonial architecture in Santa Fe. Christopher Wilson, in his architectural and cultural history of the Plaza, noted that they are "the only pre-1880 sites to survive modernization to the point of not losing their original character."

Prince Plaza (or Trujillos Plaza as it is sometimes called) was the first office of the Manhattan Project of 1943 (now the U.S. Atomic Energy Commission). When the first scientists working on the atomic bomb arrived in Santa Fe, they checked in at the office in Prince Plaza before being transferred to Los Alamos ranch. Today the plaza contains a restaurant, offices and shops.

Sena heirs sold the property to Martha and Amelia White in 1927. The sisters hired William Penhallow Henderson to remodel and restore it. The second stories on the east and north were added at that time.

THEN — COUNTY COURTHOUSE
EAST PALACE AVENUE, ca. 1907-1908

The need for a new County courthouse prompted County Commissioner Bernard Seligman's proposal that it be built in the middle of the Plaza, leaving a city park on four sides, a plan used by many American cities in the 1880s. Public outcry against the proposal resulted in its construction on East Palace Avenue. The site had been a roller skating rink in the late 1860s. In earlier days it had been a cienega or swamp. The water table was, and still is, very high here. Acequias had furnished domestic and irrigation water for that section of the city, including the Palace of the Governors. It was this water supply which both the Indians and General de Vargas cut off to gain entrance to the Palace.

Construction of the courthouse began in 1886-87 at a cost of $53,000 in a German municipal style. On February 8, 1909, a fire gutted the structure and it was rebuilt in 1910.

NE3

NOW — CORONADO BUILDING,
EAST PALACE AVENUE

In 1940 Henry Dendahl, merchant and banker, purchased the courthouse property and began construction of a new building of Spanish Colonial style.

THEN — TERRACE BAR & BOWLING
729 EAST PALACE AVENUE

The J.J. Stoner map of 1882 and Sanborn Insurance map of 1890 show this location belonging to the Fisher Brewing Co., owned by Adolph Fisher. An ice plant was constructed across the street from the brewery in 1890 and river water was used both for making beer and ice. It was Santa Fe's first ice plant and produced 6,000 pounds daily. The ice was stored in caves in the hill behind the tap room.

NE4

NOW — 729 EAST PALACE AVENUE
(private residence)

The Honorable Aloysius B. Renahan, a local attorney and member of the Santa Fe Ring, purchased the property, and Terrace Bar and Bowling became a thing of the past. He remodeled the structure into a home named "The Willows." East Palace Avenue became the area where the wealthy and influential lived. Mrs. Marrietta Dodge Phelps Lord Renahan continued to live in the home after her husband's death in 1928 until 1964, when she passed on.

THEN — PALACE HOTEL, ca. 1880-1883

With the coming of the railroad in1880, Santa Fe businessmen recognized the need for a hotel for arriving tourists in addition to the old Exchange Hotel. The result was the Palace Hotel. Many western towns had a "Palace Hotel," rather like the Holiday Inns of today, where a newcomer could get a good meal and a comfortable bed.

The Palace was wooden construction, flimsy and inexpensive. Designed in the Second Empire style, it had a mansard roof and ornate wrought iron.

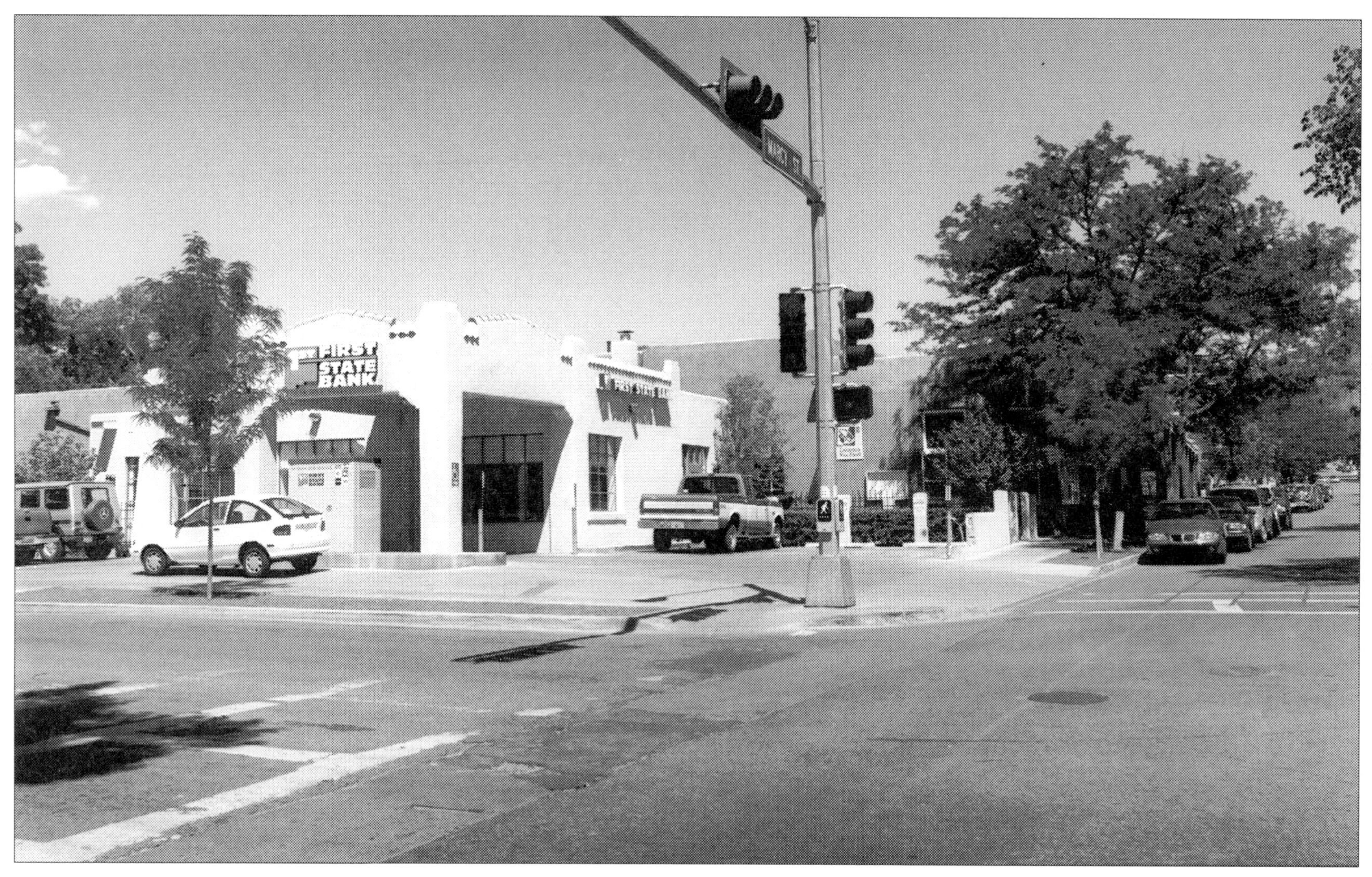

NE5

NOW — NORTHEAST CORNER,
WASHINGTON & MARCY STREETS

In 1915, the Palace Hotel was renamed the De Vargas Hotel. While being remodeled into a Spanish-Pueblo Revival design, it burned to the ground in January 1922. Since then the property has undergone successive changes with the population growth and its changing needs. The Palace, ladies in floor-length gowns and fine carriages have all disappeared in the rush of today's traffic, and nothing is left to provide a hint of its romantic past.

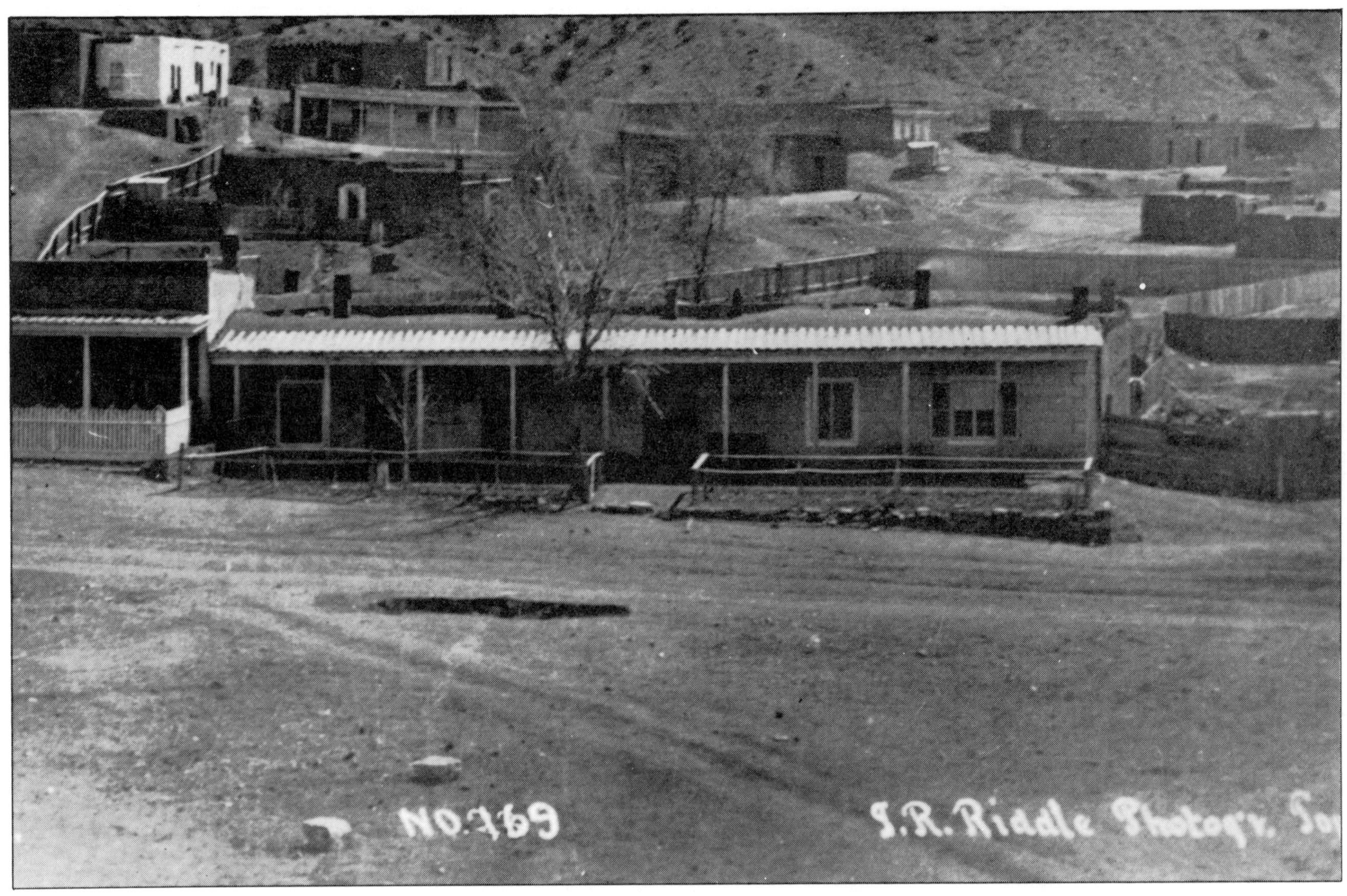

THEN — PADRE GALLEGOS HOUSE, ca. 1880

A defrocked priest, José Manuel Gallegos, noted for his love of dancing, gambling and political activities, constructed the original house in 1857 (center). A flamboyant and controversial figure, Gallegos served as Superintendent of Indian Affairs in 1868 and Speaker of the House in the territorial legislature for four terms beginning in 1857, when he moved to Santa Fe. When he died in 1875, the *Daily New Mexican* termed Gallegos "the most universally known man in the Territory."

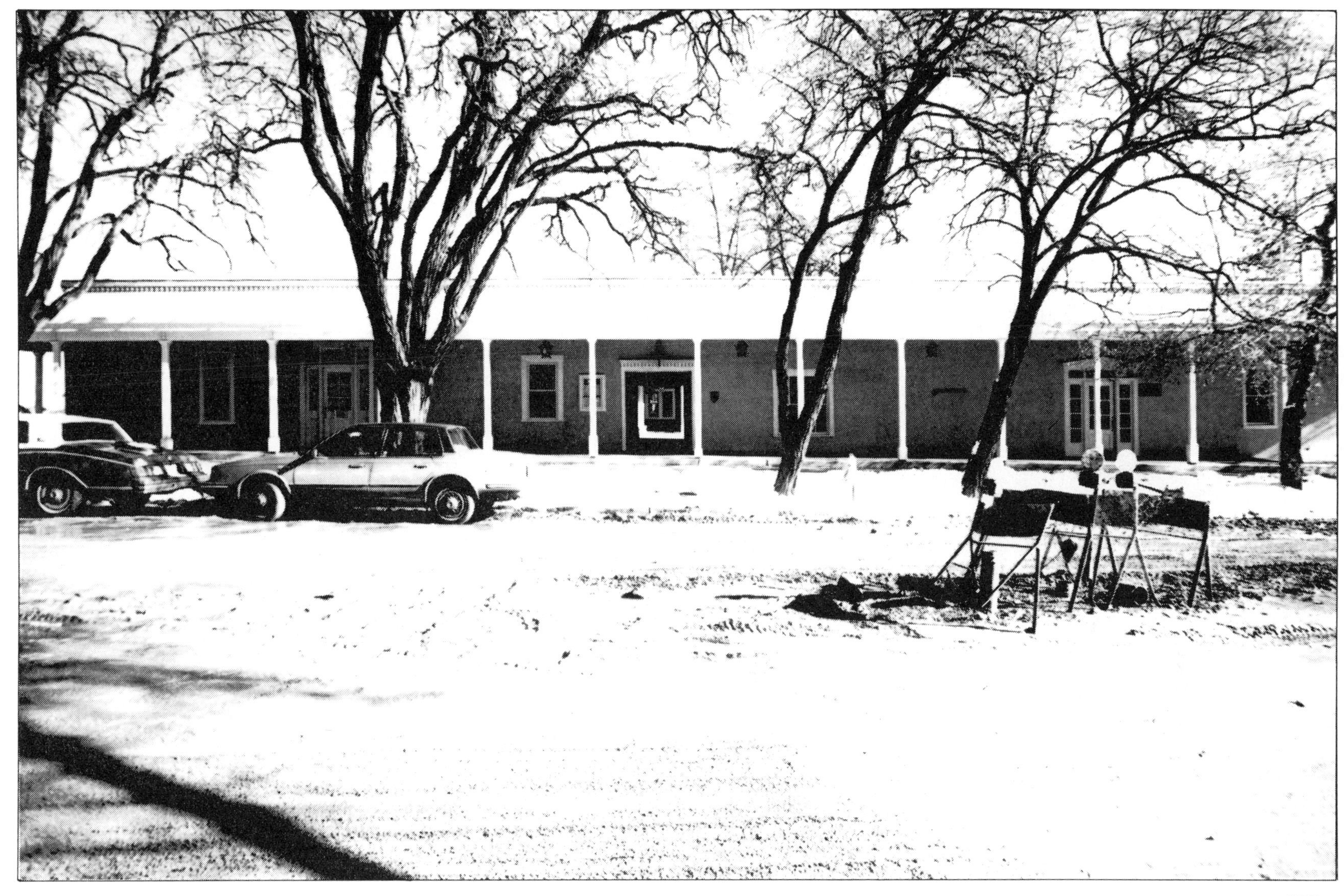

NE6

NOW — 227–237 WASHINGTON AVENUE

During the Civil War the Gallegos home was used as a rooming house and, in 1868, the First Episcopal Church of Santa Fe held services in the north wing. Sheldon Parsons, an important Santa Fe artist, lived in the house with his daughter about 1914. The house was enlarged and remodeled several times. The last remodeling occurred in 1966-67 and today is an especially nice example of Territorial architecture with a lovely placita.

THEN — THE BISHOP'S LODGE, 1928

In 1928, it was Santa Fe's first golf course. The first owner to live on the property, however, was Archbishop Jean Baptiste Lamy, the first archbishop of Santa Fe, who purchased the land in 1853. Lamy was the first French vicar in Santa Fe and his diocese included New Mexico, Arizona and Colorado. The clergy was declining when Lamy first arrived in 1851 and he set about to strengthen the church by recruiting priests from Europe and from various teaching orders for the establishment of schools. When he retired here to a small home with a private chapel in 1885, he had been elevated to archbishop, served a total of 34 years, built 85 new churches, increased the diocese to 150 churches and established several schools and hospitals.

Lamy was an amateur horticulturalist and imported many varieties of flowers and fruit trees for his gardens at The Bishop's Lodge and St. Francis Cathedral. Willa Cather's famous novel, *Death Comes for the Archbishop,* published in 1929, was based on Bishop Lamy's life. Upon his death in 1888 he was buried beneath the sanctuary of his beloved Cathedral in Santa Fe.

NE7

NOW — THE BISHOP'S LODGE

James R. Thorpe, of Denver and Minneapolis, purchased the land from two sisters who had bought the property from Archbishop Salpointe, Lamy's successor, in 1917. Thorpe began constructing resort facilities for Santa Fe visitors and called it The Bishop's Lodge. In 1922, representatives from seven western states along with Herbert Hoover, Secretary of Commerce, met at the Lodge to negotiate the Colorado River Compact which designates water regulation and use of the Colorado River.

Lamy's chapel has been preserved and is open to the public. The lodge, now an exclusive summer resort, provides vacationers with elegant and quiet seclusion.

San Francisco Street looking east to La Parroquia, ca. 1865

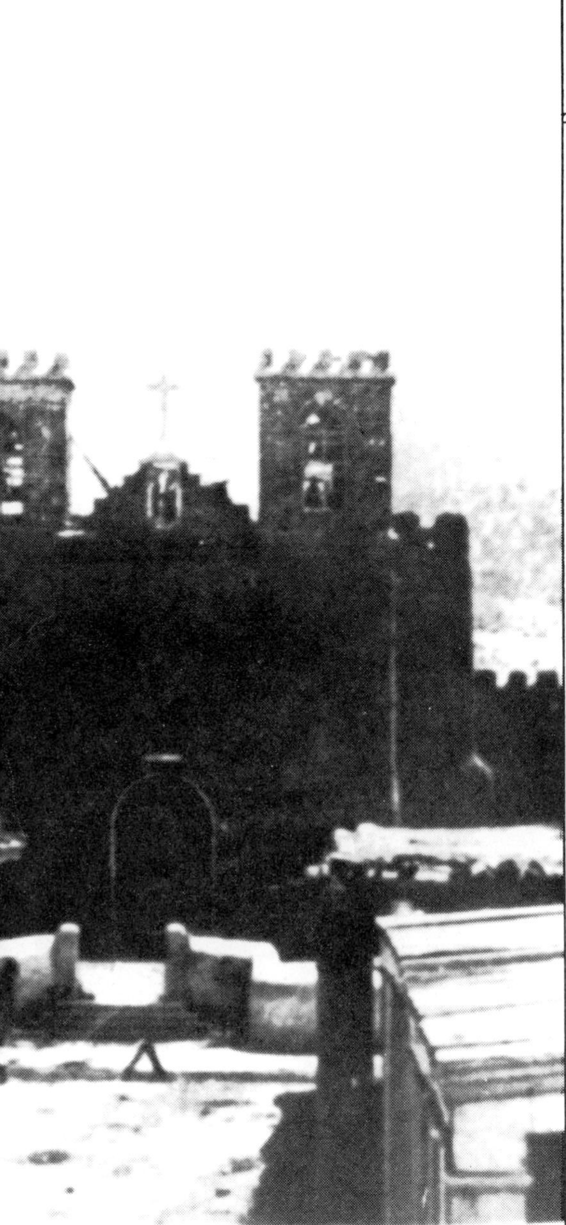

SOUTHEAST

SE1

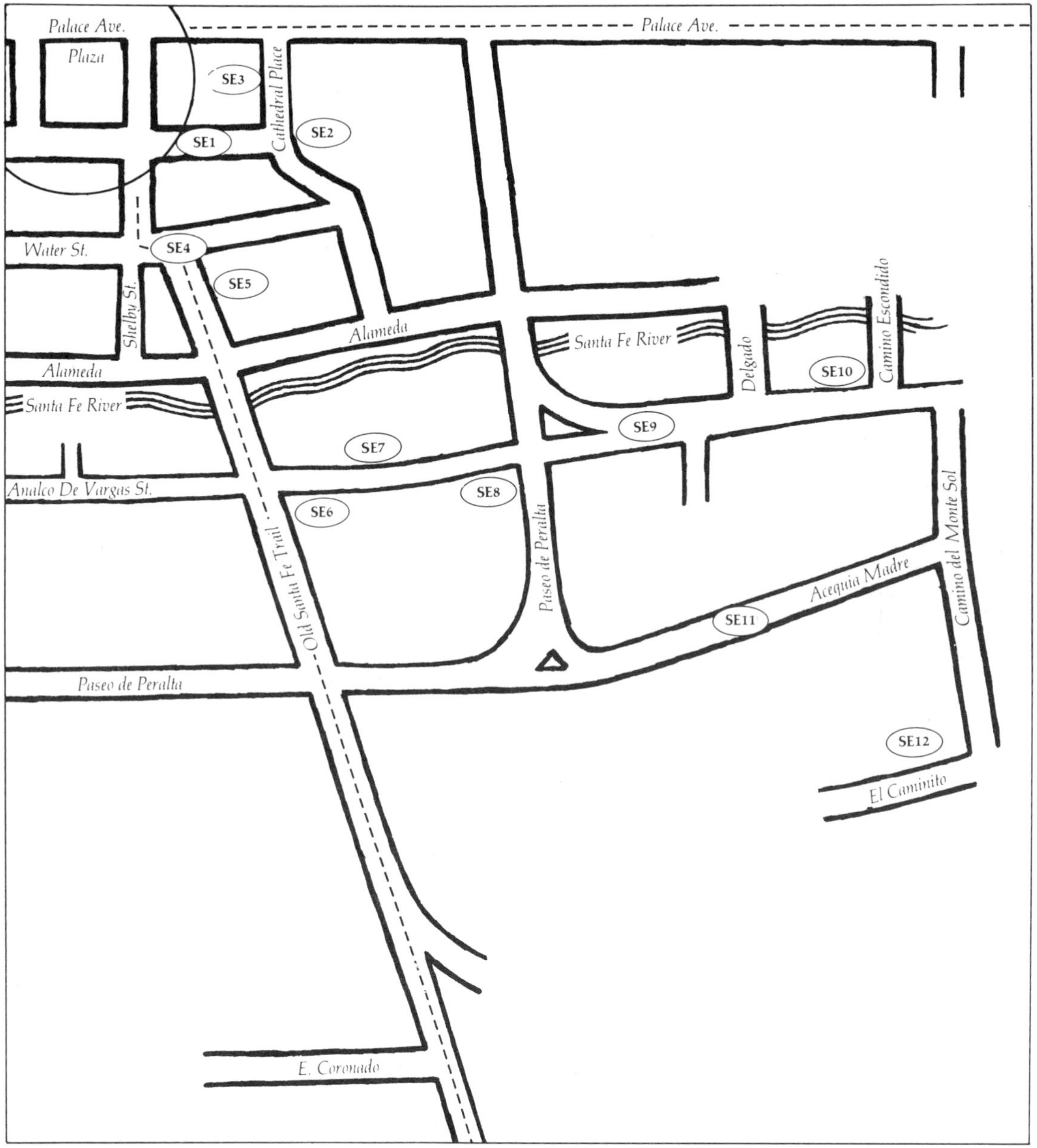

Palace Ave.
Plaza
Palace Ave.
SE3
Cathedral Place
SE1
SE2
Water St.
SE4
SE5
Shelby St.
Alameda
Alameda
Santa Fe River
Santa Fe River
Delgado
SE10
Camino Escondido
SE9
SE7
Analco De Vargas St.
SE8
SE6
Old Santa Fe Trail
Paseo de Peralta
Camino del Monte Sol
Acequia Madre
SE11
Paseo de Peralta
SE12
El Caminito
E. Coronado

THEN — ST. FRANCIS CATHEDRAL, 1900

A church has existed on this site since 1626. It was originally a parish church and formed the eastern boundary of the Plaza. During the Pueblo Revolt of 1680, the original edifice was destroyed and it was rebuilt in 1714-17, known as La Parroquia. The Conquistadora chapel was built at that time to house a small wooden statue representing the Assumption of Our Lady, first brought to Santa Fe in 1625. When the Spanish army and colonists fled south to escape the warring Pueblos, they took the statue with them. She returned with the settlers and General de Vargas and his army in 1693. She was renamed "La Conquistadora" and given credit by the thankful Spanish for the reconquest of Santa Fe.

Archbishop Lamy ordered construction of the French Romanesque cathedral in 1869. It was the first cathedral west of the Mississippi and north of Durango, Mexico. It was built around the old adobe church which was then dismantled brick by brick. The debris was carried out the main entrance to form the terrace surrounding the Cathedral. The Conquistadora chapel, on the north, is the only remnant of La Parroquia.

SE2

NOW — ST. FRANCIS CATHEDRAL

The Cathedral's exterior was completed by 1884, but work went on inside for years after that. Lamy's original plans for the cathedral called for steeples 160 feet high on the twin towers but they were never built. Each archbishop since Lamy's time has contributed to the Cathedral's decoration, renovation or enlargement. The chapel on the south was enlarged and modernized in 1966-67.

La Conquistadora continues to be carried in a religious procession on the first Sunday after the Feast of Corpus Christi each June. From the Cathedral the procession winds through town to the Rosario Cemetery Chapel. A novena of masses is said and then the oldest Madonna in the U.S. is returned to her permanent home in the Cathedral.

THEN — CATHEDRAL PLACE, ca. 1915

Carter H. Harrison, former mayor of Chicago, made several trips with his family to Santa Fe beginning in 1915 in an effort to aid his son's health. He made this photograph around that time, showing the row of old homes lining Cathedral Place. Maps of 1882 and 1890 indicate the property as residences but local legend says it was a monastery at one time.

Rosemary Nusbaum in her book, *The City Different and The Palace,* states that in 1909 the first structure was a red brick schoolhouse, the second was a two-story adobe and the last a home belonging to James Seligman. When these structures were torn down about 1919, the last three placitas on that block, and the few remaining in the city center, were destroyed.

SE3

NOW — CATHEDRAL PLACE

At the same time the Fine Arts Museum and La Fonda were being built, the Treasury Department ordered construction of a new post office on Cathedral Place. It was finished in 1922. The estimate for the concrete and brick structure was $200,000, but an April 1, 1922, article in the *New Mexican* quoted the cost as $300,000. The design included two open courtyards reminiscent, perhaps, of the former placitas. Today, it is the site of the Institute of American Indian Arts Museum.

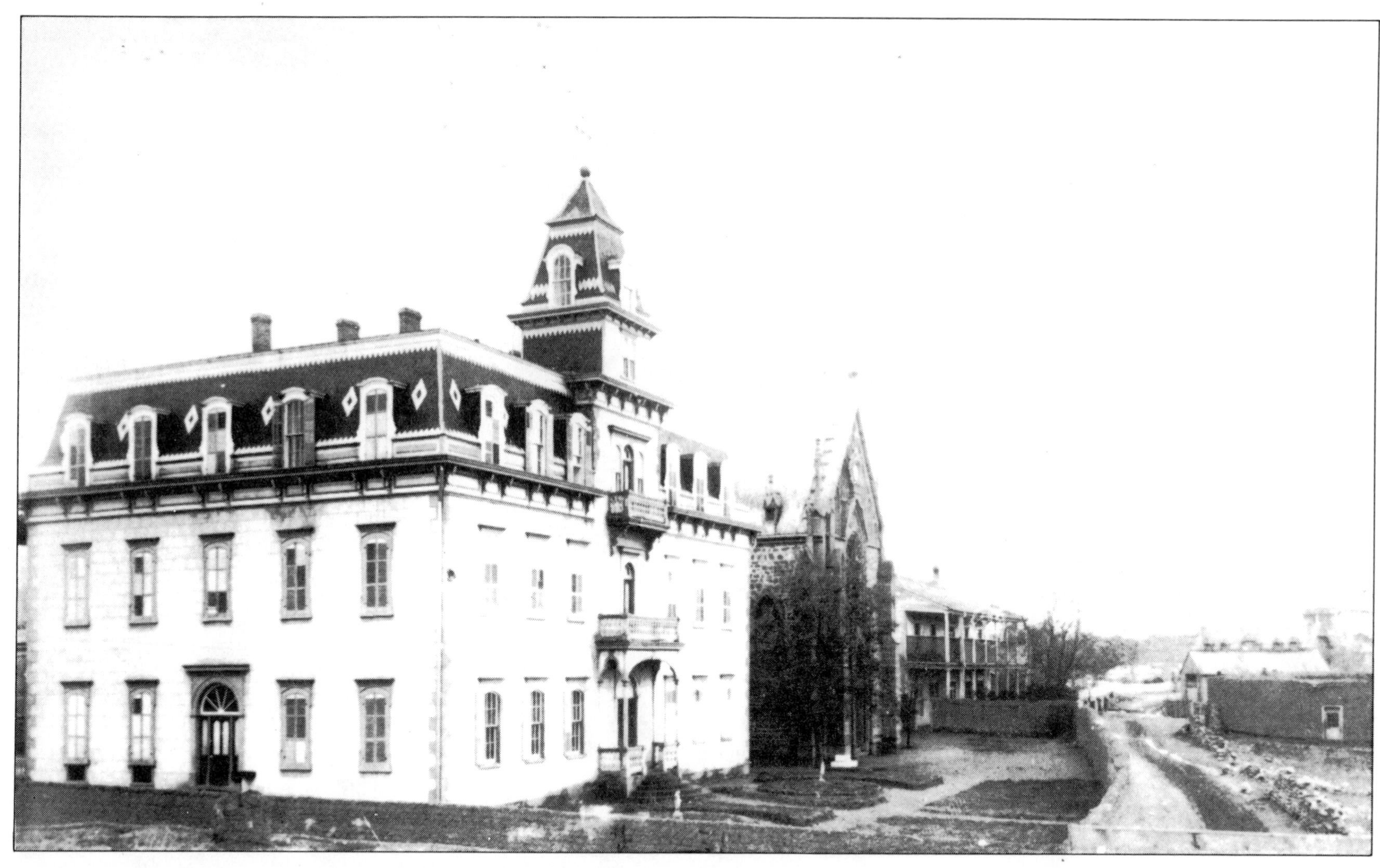

THEN — OLD SANTA FE TRAIL, ca. 1885

Six nuns of the Order of Loretto in Kentucky arrived in Santa Fe in 1852 at the request of Archbishop Lamy. They were the first women's religious order in New Mexico. Over a period of four years they acquired four and a half acres on College Street, as it became known, on which to build a school, chapel and convent.

The large white building was the school, erected in 1880. It had a mansard roof and was built out of locally made brick. Next was the chapel dedicated to Our Lady of Light. The third building was the convent. Over the years several other buildings were constructed to the rear, including a gymnasium.

On the far right of the picture is the square tower of San Miguel Mission and the cupola of the Christian Brothers Academy, the school for boys. In 1968, the Loretto Academy was closed and its students merged with those at St. Michael's High School.

SE4

NOW — OLD SANTA FE TRAIL

College Street has been renamed Old Santa Fe Trail (which it always was) and today only the Chapel of Loretto remains. In 1971 the entire property was sold for commercial development and all the buildings but the Chapel were razed. The Inn at Loretto was constructed in 1973-1975 in Spanish-Pueblo Revival style. It is connected to the chapel, forming an interesting entrance and comparison of architectural styles.

THEN — LORETTO CHAPEL, ca. 1880-81
(Chapel of Our Lady of Light)

George C. Bennett photographed the Loretto Chapel in the early 1880s, mislabeling it "St. Mary's Chapel." Construction by French stonemasons was begun under orders from Archbishop Lamy in January 1873, and completed in 1878. Of all the construction in Santa Fe going on during those years, it was the only stone building to be completed by 1880, when the railroad arrived.

This photo reveals some particularly interesting details. The stone used for construction hadn't yet been plastered over and the circular window at the top is missing. It would be eight more years before the three-foot iron statue of Our Lady of Lourdes would be placed atop the spire.

At the top of the low building to the right is a rectangular relief which Archbishop Lamy salvaged from the entrance of La Castrense (the military chapel on the Plaza). The relief is particularly beautiful and may be seen today in the reredo (bottom center panel) at Cristo Rey Church.

Bennett left us a singular memento in this photograph, instructive to all students of photography. At the very bottom, right side, appearing against the wall, is his shadow!

SE5

NOW — LORETTO CHAPEL

The graceful Gothic lines of the chapel are just as beautiful today as they were 100 years ago. The interior, evidencing French influences, is exquisite with its white altar and beautifully adorned sanctuary. Today it is used only for small weddings. It is administered by the Sisters of Loretto but maintained by the Historic Santa Fe Foundation.

The chapel is best known for the unique spiral staircase at the rear of the building. When the chapel was completed in 1878, workmen had left no way to ascend to the choir loft. It was felt the floorplan had accidentally omitted sufficient room to build an ordinary staircase. The Sisters prayed for a solution to the dilemma and shortly thereafter a carpenter appeared. Using wood not from a local source and only wooden pegs for nails, he built a circular staircase without any center support -- an engineering marvel and just as "miraculous" today as when it was built. He left without asking for payment.

The railing was added at a later time by a local carpenter. In the interest of preservation, the staircase is no longer used.

Legend has attributed the staircase to St. Joseph, the carpenter saint. Contrasting research indicates it was possibly the work of an Austrian immigrant who was visiting the area and learned of the Sisters' need.

Old Church & College

No. 172

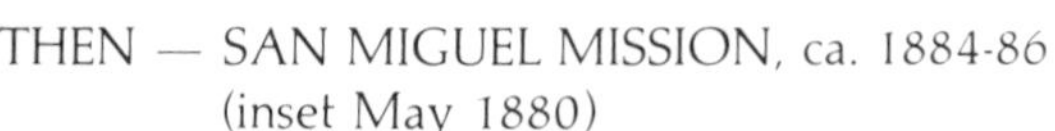

THEN — SAN MIGUEL MISSION, ca. 1884-86
(inset May 1880)

When Fray Alonso de Benavides arrived in Santa Fe in 1626 with the small wooden statue, La Conquistadora, the San Miguel church was already in use. Its original construction probably dates back to 1610-12.

J.R. Riddle's photograph shows the church in a state of disrepair, which it frequently was in the course of its 370 years. The three-tiered bell tower of the early 19th century had collapsed.

It was rebuilt in 1887 with a square tower and shuttered louvers. Note the lack of buttresses, which were added to the exterior later on to keep the walls from collapsing.

San Miguel was a parish church, built to serve the religious needs of the Indian laborers brought from Mexico by the Spanish. It is built entirely of adobe brick. The structure seen today dates back to 1710, the year inscribed on the main beam of the choir loft. The massive walls and high windows made the church a stronghold against attack.

The large building to the right of San Miguel was St. Michael's High School, built in 1878. It became a landmark in the city because it was the highest adobe structure in Santa Fe. Another of Archbishop Lamy's projects, the boys' school was operated by the Christian Brothers, an order brought to Santa Fe by Lamy in 1859.

NOW — SAN MIGUEL MISSION

The oldest church in the U.S. still in use is now refurbished, stuccoed and painted adobe color. When you enter San Miguel, you see a wonderful example of an 18th-century New Mexico church, containing the same religious art seen in the 1880 interior. The reredo (altar screen) is the oldest wooden reredo in Santa Fe, made in 1798. The 17th-and 18th-century paintings, some on deer and buffalo hide, and carved statue of St. Michael provide an atmosphere of authenticity and antiquity.

THEN — THE OLDEST HOUSE, ca. 1881
(inset ca. 1912)

Tradition has labeled it the "oldest house in Santa Fe." It appears on the J.J. Stoner map of 1882 as "the oldest building in Santa Fe," and a structure across from San Miguel appears on the José Urrutia map of 1766-68. The archaeologist Adolph Bandelier believed the origins of the house dated back to 1250 A.D.

SE7

and the Tiwa Indian pueblo of Analco. In 1905, Dr. Edgar Lee Hewett, Director of the School of American Research, agreed with Bandelier's conclusion. Tree-ring specimens taken from the vigas in the ceilings date from 1740-67.

NOW — THE OLDEST HOUSE

In 1881 the property was purchased by the Brothers of the Christian Schools (also known as the Christian Brothers), who also own and maintain San Miguel Mission. The house has been open to the public since that time.

In 1902 the second story, structurally unsound, was removed. It was rebuilt 25 years later.

The east end of the house is operated as a gift shop. The west end remains the last example of what was once construction typical of the Barrio district: hand-formed adobe walls, a dirt floor, a tiny, low window and a ceiling of latillas and vigas (small poles and logs). The merging of Indian and Spanish architectural styles, once common in Spanish settlements, died out under United States jurisdiction from 1846 on.

THEN — JOSÉ ALARÍD HOUSE, ca. 1910
338 East De Vargas

Records regarding this house date back to 1835 when José Alaríd purchased the property. He constructed the home after that date. Alaríd was a disabled veteran of the Mexican Army stationed at the Santa Fe Presidio. He later sold the house to Joseph Hersch in 1854. Five years later it was sold to Archbishop Lamy. Lamy's use of the house isn't known. The house was again sold in 1864 to Epifanio Vigil, who was territorial auditor from 1865 to 1869 and official interpreter in 1868.

SE8

NOW — 338 EAST DE VARGAS

Among the prominent Santa Fe owners of this property was Anita J. Chapman, the eldest daughter of James L. Johnson (who owned El Zaguán and the Johnson Block on the Plaza). Mrs. Chapman acquired the home in 1911. She worked as Adolph Bandelier's secretary and translator, and later was the first woman to become territorial librarian and finally state librarian from 1917 to 1937.

THEN — CANYON ROAD, ca. 1910

The Spanish called it "el camino del cañon" (the road of the canyon). Indian pueblos may have existed in Santa Fe (near the present-day Sears building and the Barrio de Analco district) in the 1200s. Their location within the boundaries of the city has never been accurately determined. Canyon Road was a trail leading up the Santa Fe River, across the Sangre de Cristo Mountains to Pecos Pueblo on the other side.

The 1768 map of Santa Fe by José Urrutia shows Canyon Road as a residential area as does the 1846 Gilmer map. Some of the homes seen today date back to early territorial days (1846-56) and a few to the late 1700s.

Woodcutters coming from the Sangre de Cristos used the road until early in this century. Burros heaped with firewood, selling door-to-door, were a common sight in the city.

SE9

NOW — CANYON ROAD

The 1920s were renaissance years for the arts in America. Writers and artists began to infiltrate the Canyon Road area during that time. Many came to regain their health in Santa Fe's mild climate at Sunmount Sanitorium.
Once recovered, they stayed. Among the artists living on Canyon Road or Camino del Monte Sol were Willard Nash, Will Shuster, Josef Bakos, Walter Mruk, Fremont Ellis, Gerald Cassidy, Randall Davey, Sheldon Parsons, William Penhallow Henderson and Olive Rush. Several others of note (Henry C. Balink, Gustave Baumann and John Sloan, to name a few) settled a little closer to town.

Today the Olive Rush home (630 Canyon Road) belongs to the Santa Fe Society of Friends (Quakers). The Randall Davey home (1655 Canyon road), originally Santa Fe's first lumber mill, has been given to the National Audubon Society.

Current artists and superb craftsmen of all kinds display their wares in the shops, galleries and restaurants along the Road, the oldest road still in use in America.

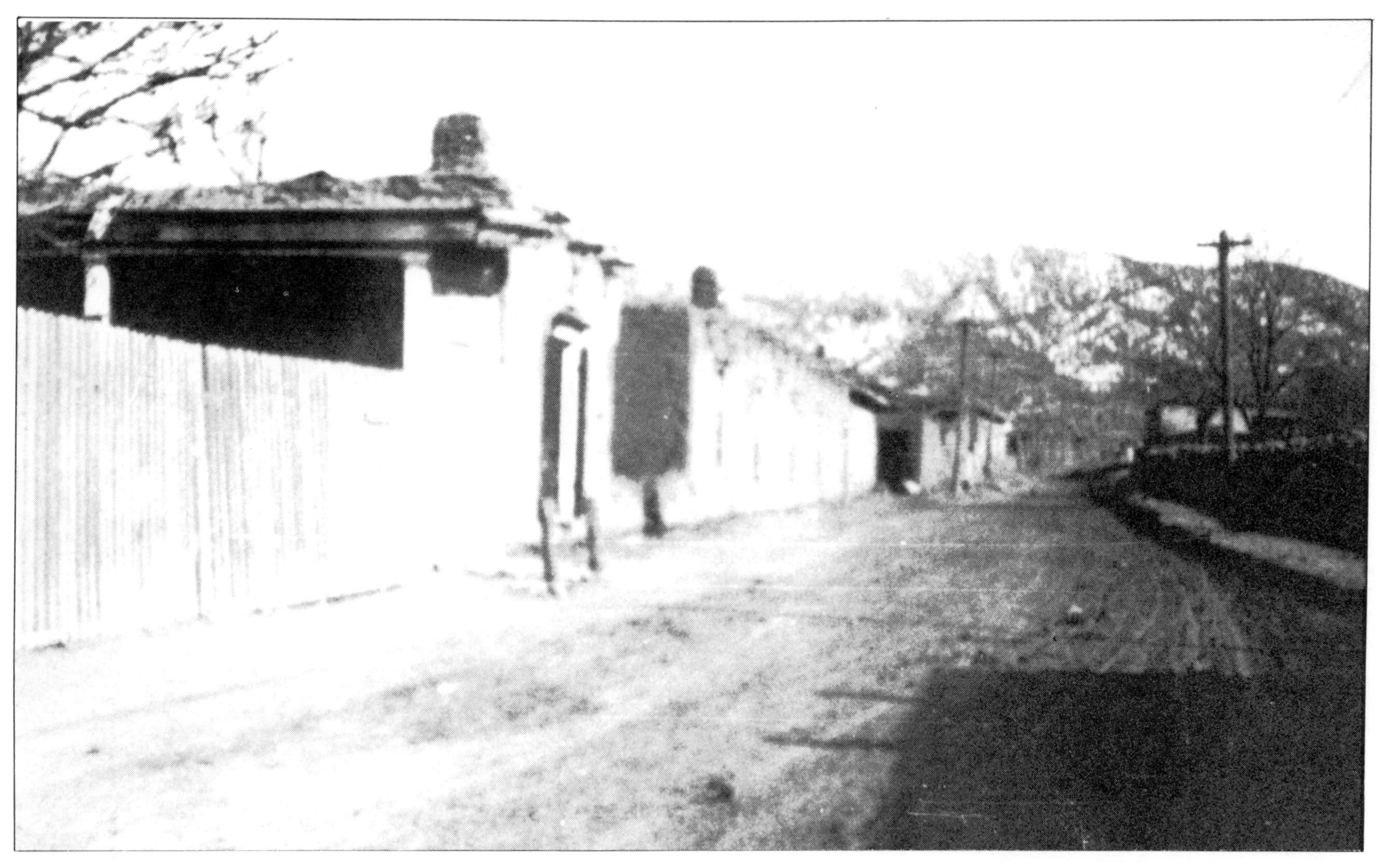

THEN — EL ZAGUÁN, ca. 1917
545 Canyon Road

The name means a roofed space or corridor joining separate buildings or rooms. The passageway runs the entire length of the house. It was purchased in 1849 by James L. Johnson, the merchant who later built the Johnson Block on the northeast side of the Plaza. Johnson added to the existing two or three rooms, which had walls four feet thick, until it totaled nineteen rooms in all. Being a prosperous merchant, Johnson designated one room as the "treasure room" for storing the family valuables. Another was a private chapel, and a third was called the "chocolate room" because chocolate was ground and served there in the afternoons, after the Mexican custom. Adolph Bandelier, the archaeologist and a family friend, laid out the garden on the west end. It includes horse chestnuts planted by Johnson in 1850 and peony bushes imported from China.

SE10

NOW — EL ZAGUÁN (private apartments)

Colonel James Baca, Johnson's grandson, was the last family member to own El Zaguán, selling it in 1927. By the 30s, Margretta S. Dietrich had purchased the place and it became a private girls' school known as Brownmoor. It was after this time that the house was remodeled into rental apartments.

In 1979 the Historic Santa Fe Foundation purchased the property for preservation purposes. The exterior has changed little since the old photo was taken. The old well still remains under the back portal.

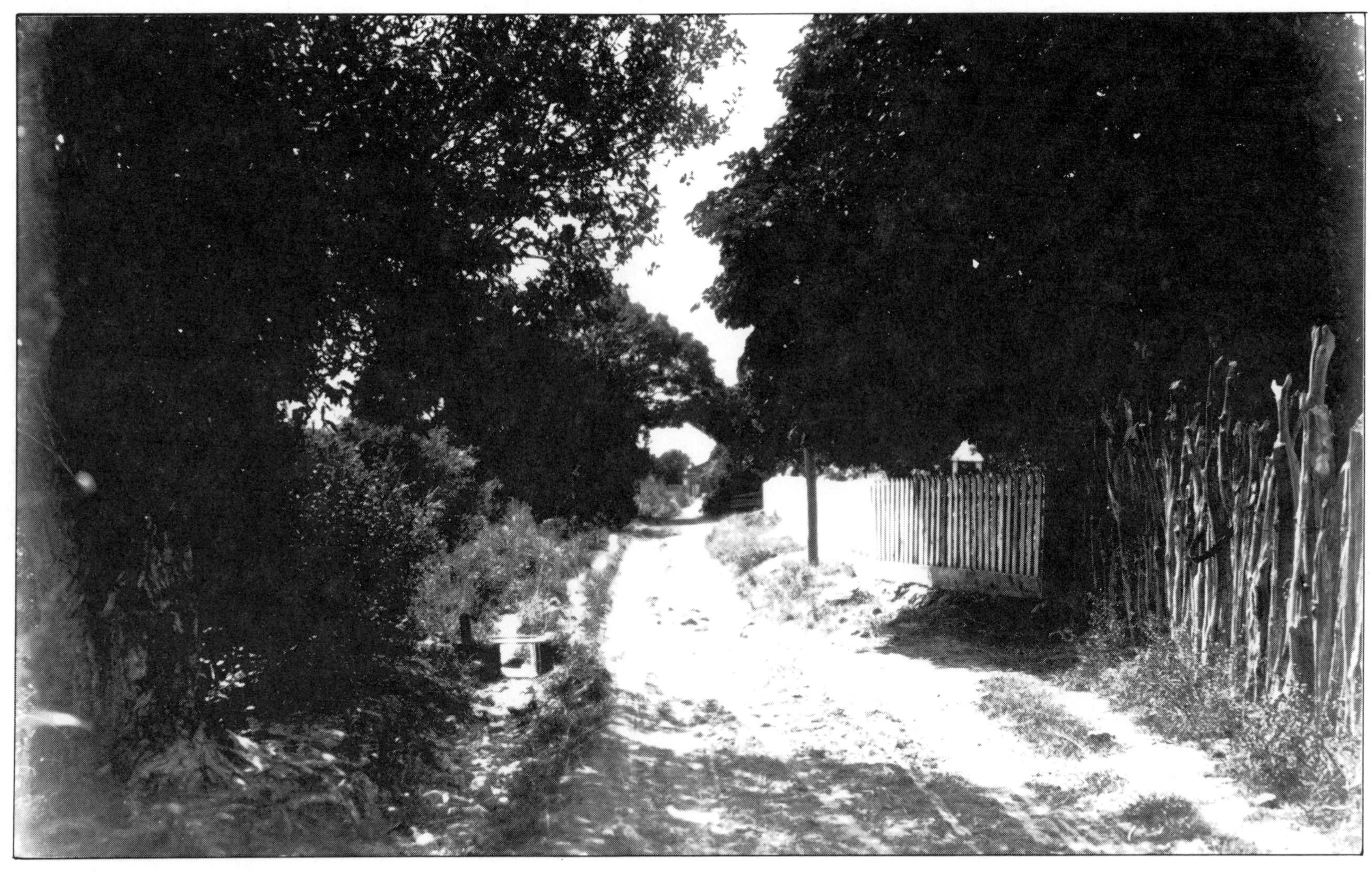

THEN — ACEQUIA MADRE, ca. 1912

From 1909 to 1912, Jesse Nusbaum, photographer and staff member at the Museum of New Mexico, made a detailed photographic survey of Santa Fe. His photograph of Acequia Madre reveals the quiet mood of that residential area to the southeast of the city. Coyote fences (vertical poles), shade trees, gardens and dusty roads were typical then. The leisurely lifestyle of Santa Fe encouraged newcomers seeking a different way of living to stay.

Acequia Madre means "mother ditch." Water is diverted from the Santa Fe River. The Tlaxcalan Indians living in the Barrio de Analco district depended on the ditch for irrigating their corn fields. Many other acequias operated in Santa Fe during Spanish colonial times as noted on early maps. Although Pueblo Indians used irrigation, the Spanish brought engineering knowledge and practical irrigation law to the new colony, which were necessary for the development and regulation of water systems.

SE11

NOW — ACEQUIA MADRE

Only a portion of the road is left unpaved today, but many of the residential streets in the area remain dirt because of public demand. Santa Feans are protective not only of their historic buildings and landmarks but also of the traditional relaxed lifestyle which makes Santa Fe so pleasing today.

The mother ditch is still used today, governed by a mayordomo (manager). A tax to residents holding water rights pays for its maintenance. It is the last remaining acequia in Santa Fe which is clearly visible and operational.

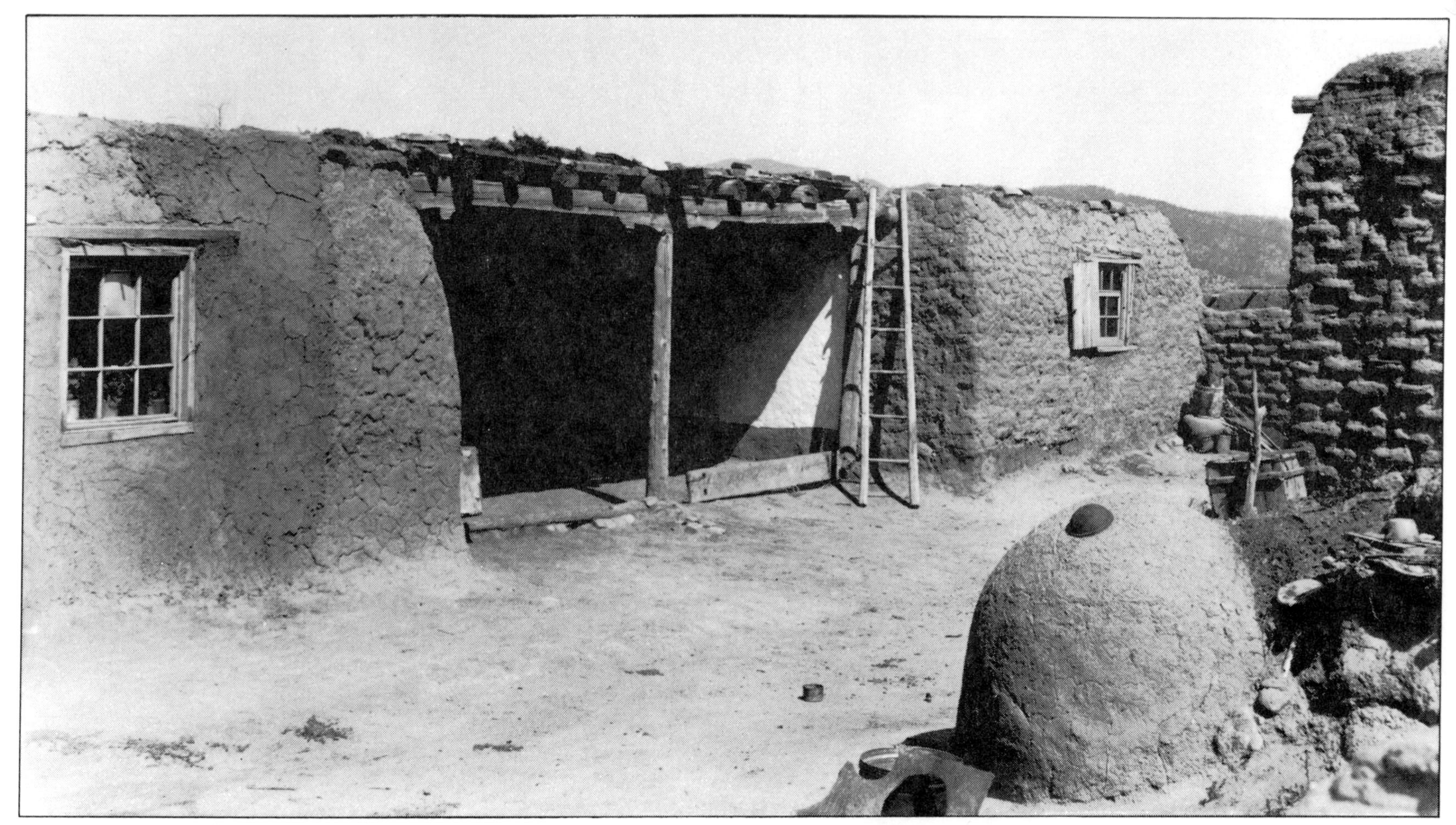

THEN — DE LA PEÑA HOUSE, 1912
831 El Caminito

Jesse Nusbaum photographed the house when it was still owned by the de la Peña family, who had occupied it for almost 80 years. The horno (outdoor oven) in the foreground was the traditional summer Indian-style stove used for family cooking. In winter, when warmth was wanted inside the house, a fireplace was used.

Sergeant Francisco de la Peña purchased the property in 1845 for 114 pesos. It consisted of farm ground and a house of four rooms with a portal. De la Peña was a soldier in the presidial companies of both Santa Fe and San Miguel and served in several compaigns against the Indians as well as in peace negotiations with the Navajos in 1835.

SE12

NOW — DE LA PEÑA HOUSE
(private residence)

When Isabilita Rodriguez de la Peña died in 1909, the house and property were divided among the six surviving children. Each received some land, six vigas of the house (the old style of apportionment) and the right of entry and exit to it.

Two de la Peña daughters remained in the house when Frank G. Applegate purchased the house and land in 1925-26. Applegate was a well-known writer and artist who took an interest in local crafts and, along with friend and fellow author Mary Austin, contributed to the preservation of several New Mexico mission churches.

Applegate remodeled and enlarged the house, adding a second story with a Spanish Colonial balcony with beams and corbels taken from an old building. Great care was taken to add several authentic details to the interior. Today it is a lovely example of an early 19th-century Spanish-Pueblo home.

The Plaza looking west toward Lincoln Avenue, ca. 1866

SOUTHWEST

SW1

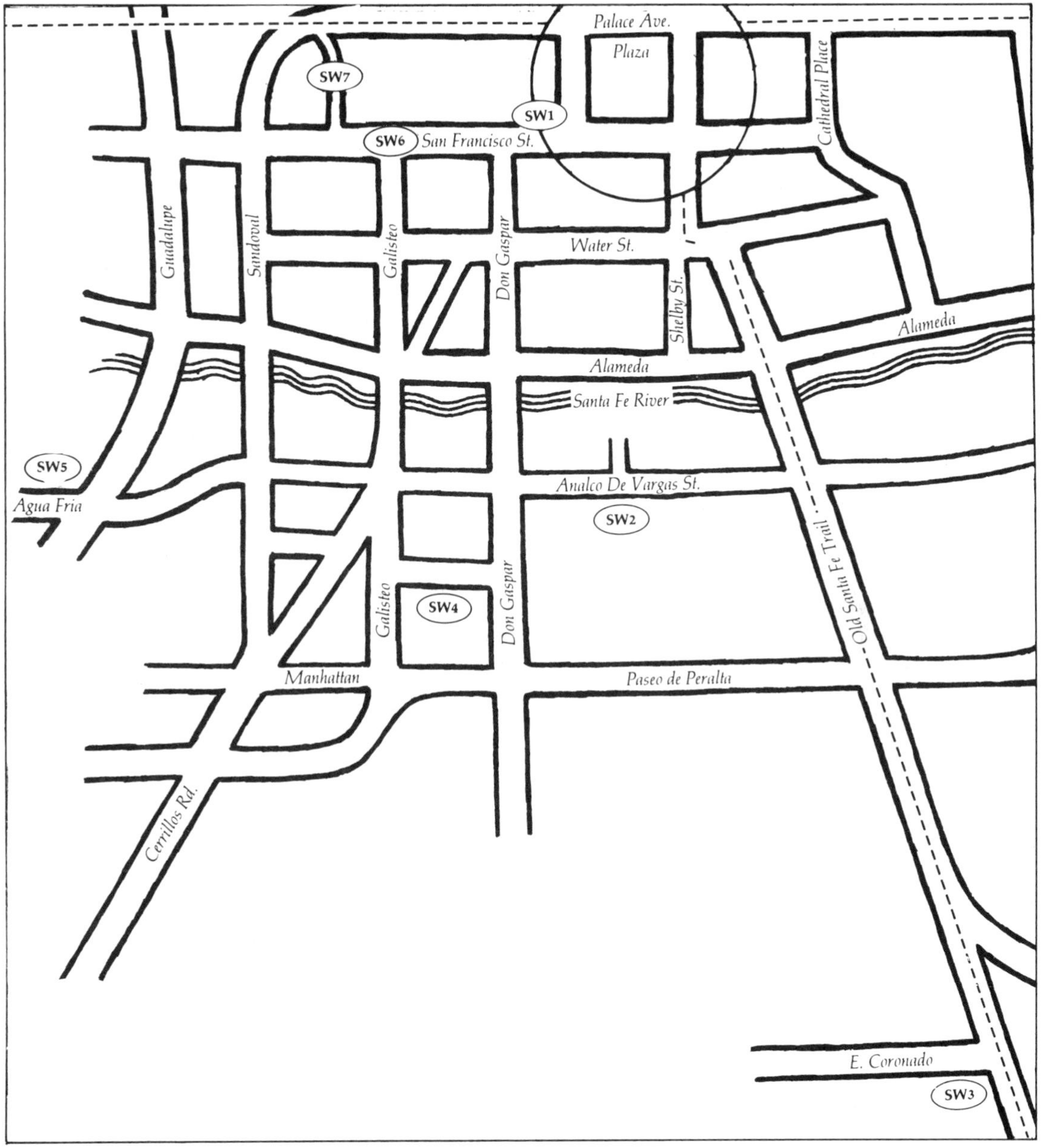

Palace Ave.
Plaza
SW7
SW1
SW6 San Francisco St.
Cathedral Place
Guadalupe
Sandoval
Galisteo
Don Gaspar
Water St.
Shelby St.
Alameda
Alameda
Santa Fe River
SW5
Agua Fria
Analco De Vargas St.
SW2
Galisteo
SW4
Don Gaspar
Old Santa Fe Trail
Manhattan
Paseo de Peralta
Cerrillos Rd.
E. Coronado
SW3

THEN — ANALCO STREET, ca. 1879-81

Ben Wittick was a prolific photographer who photographed much of the West, including Santa Fe. He visited Santa Fe in the late 1870s and returned again about 1900. His photograph looks east toward San Miguel Mission, the heart of Barrio de Analco.

To quote *Old Santa Fe Today,* the Barrio district is "the oldest settlement of European origin in Santa Fe except for the Plaza, and hence one of the oldest in the United States." Originally it was inhabited by Tlaxcalan Indian servants brought from Mexico by the Spanish officials and Franciscan missionaries. It extended from

SW2

San Miguel to Hancock Street (near Sandoval today). "Analco" means "the other side of the water" and referred to the fact that the settlement was across the Santa Fe River from the Plaza, the official buildings and the homes of prominent citizens. Early Santa Fe was clearly divided into *los ricos y los pobres,* the rich and the poor.

By the 1770s the Barrio, razed and sacked during the Pueblo Revolt, had been rebuilt and was occupied by married soldiers, *genizaros* (Indians living as Europeans) and artisans.

NOW — DE VARGAS STREET

Analco Street was renamed De Vargas after Governor Diego de Vargas. The mean, flat-roofed adobes and dirty streets of a hundred years ago have been replaced with exclusive Spanish-Pueblo homes secluded behind high adobe walls. Excellent restaurants and fine shops surround San Miguel, where the Spanish Market once flourished. The State Capitol and other government buildings dominate the area today. Cornfields have given way to parking lots.

THEN — CARLOS VIERRA HOUSE, 1921
1002 Old Pecos Trail

Of Portuguese descent, Carlos Vierra was a California-born artist who came to Santa Fe in 1904 to regain his health. He was the first artist to make Santa Fe his permanent home. He became interested in photography and opened a studio on the Plaza. By 1907 he had become acquainted with Dr. Edgar L. Hewett, director of the School of American Research (formerly the School of American Archaeology). He became a member of the School as well as a staff member of the Museum of New Mexico.

Vierra designed and built his own home with the financial aid of Frank Springer, a territorial senator, lawyer and patron of the arts. Vierra worked on the home for three years, from 1919 to 1921. It was carefully constructed with a Zuni-style fireplace and balcony, hand-carved beams and modelling around the doors and windows.

SW3

NOW — 1002 OLD PECOS TRAIL
(private residence)

Vierra became known as an apostle of adobe architecture. With his devotion to and development of what is now termed the "Santa Fe style," he was one of the major contributors to Spanish-Pueblo Revival architecture and had an influence on the design of the Fine Arts Museum. Vierra's best-known artwork can be seen in the Auditorium of the Fine Arts Museum. The three large murals were begun by the Utah painter Donald Beauregard. Upon Beauregard's death, they were finished by Vierra and Kenneth Chapman.

As an artist, architect, anthropologist and, later, an aerial photographer, Vierra made significant contributions to his professions. His home, now a private residence, is a lasting contribution to the city.

THEN — FIRST TERRITORIAL CAPITOL
ca. 1886

The newly constructed Capitol was a large, imposing edifice. It burned down in 1892. The cause was never determined but arson was suspected. A second, one-domed building of similar design was erected in 1900.

The 1880s were truly the end of an era in Santa Fe and much of the West. The horrendous cattle drives from Texas of the 1860s and 70s came to an end with the arrival of the railroad. Geronimo, the Chiricahua chieftain, was captured in 1886, ending the long period of Indian warfare in New Mexico. Land speculation on the public domain and Spanish land grants accelerated into a national scandal, causing great controversy and conflict. Indians became involved in the legal disputes as they struggled to preserve their traditional homelands.

SW4

NOW — BATAAN MEMORIAL BUILDING

New Mexico achieved statehood as the 47th state in 1912 after repeated attempts in 1850, 1867, 1870 and 1889. The Capitol building of 1900 was completely renovated in 1950-53. Its dome and pillars were removed and a stately Territorial design was instituted. The 1909 Governor's Mansion, located just north of the Capitol, was razed in 1955 and a new one built on Mansion Drive, north of the city. A new, round state capitol building on Paseo de Peralta opened in 1966.

New Mexico furnished hundreds of servicemen for military service in World War II. It suffered one of the highest casualty rates of all the states. The Bataan Memorial Building was dedicated to the 200th and 515th Coast Artillery Anti-aircraft Regiments stationed on the Philippines and to the survivors of the Bataan Death March.

THEN — SANTUARIO DE GUADALUPE
ca. 1880

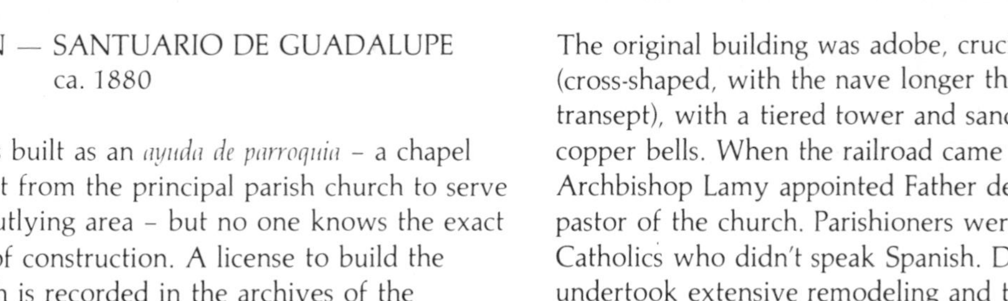

It was built as an *ayuda de parroquia* – a chapel distant from the principal parish church to serve the outlying area – but no one knows the exact date of construction. A license to build the church is recorded in the archives of the Archdiocese of Santa Fe on October 14, 1795. Construction dates are estimated from 1795 to 1807.

It was built beside El Camino Real (the Royal Road), later known as the Chihuahua Trail, the principal trade route from Vera Cruz to Mexico City to Chihuahua to Santa Fe – the oldest highway in the United States. The church was originally a shrine to the Virgin of Guadalupe, and mass was said perhaps once a month when the priest from La Parroquia would come from town.

The original building was adobe, cruciform (cross-shaped, with the nave longer than the transept), with a tiered tower and sand-cast copper bells. When the railroad came in 1880, Archbishop Lamy appointed Father de Fouri pastor of the church. Parishioners were Roman Catholics who didn't speak Spanish. De Fouri undertook extensive remodeling and transformed it from Franciscan mission style into neo-Gothic design by adding a peaked roof, steeple and Gothic windows. A fire made remodeling necessary again in 1922, this time into California mission style.

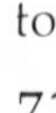

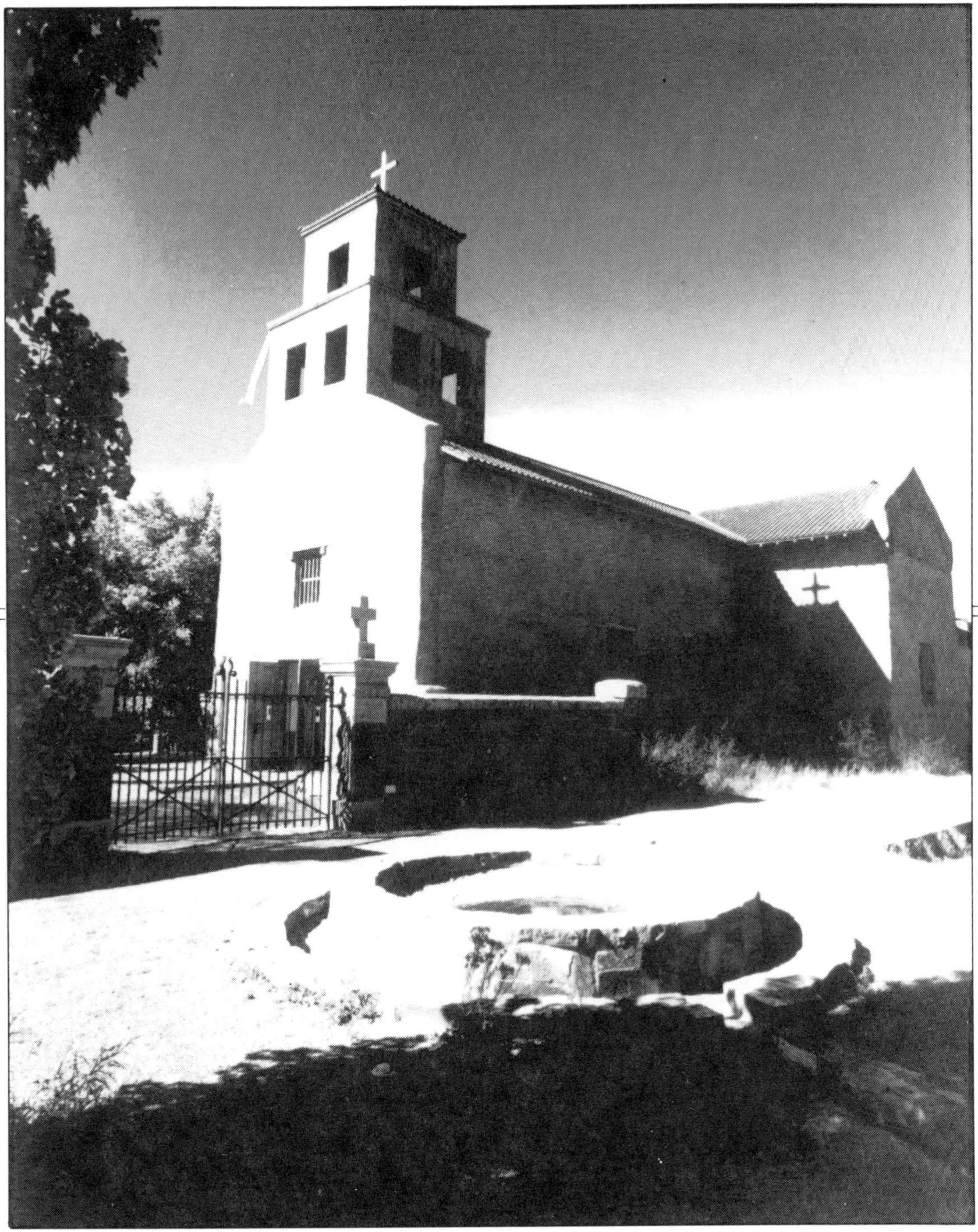

NOW — SANTUARIO DE GUADALUPE

The Santuario was deeded to the Guadalupe Historic Foundation in 1974 and was restored in 1976 to coincide with the Bicentennial. Central to its decor is the altar painting of Our Lady of Guadalupe, dated 1783 by José de Alzibar. As Alzibar was a well-known Mexican artist, it is possible that the canvas was commissioned for the church and arrived by mule caravan on El Camino Real (now Agua Fria Street), the south border of the property.

J.S.CANDELARIO.

SW6

THEN — LOWER SAN FRANCISCO STREET
ca. 1900 (inset, ca. 1920)

J.C. Candelario became one of the best-known merchants in the curio trade in all New Mexico. He was born in Albuquerque and educated in Santa Fe at St. Michael's College and Park College in Parkville, Missouri. He started his own business on lower San Francisco Street in 1890. A carreta, the traditional Pueblo ox-cart, was placed on the roof to attract attention.

The Pueblo Indians had developed basketry, pottery and weaving with cotton prior to the arrival of the Spanish. The Indians mined for turquoise near Cerrillos long before the Spanish arrived. They continued under Spanish rule, making the Cerrillos district one of the oldest continuously mined regions in the U.S. The Spanish introduced sheep and wool yarn to both Pueblos and Navajos. The native crafts were slowly being accepted as an important art form by 1900, and collectors began acquiring excellent examples of pottery, baskets, rugs and silver jewelry.

NOW — LOWER SAN FRANCISCO STREET

The 1920s brought a revival of interest in Indian crafts. Black pottery by Maria Martinez of San Ildefonso Pueblo became world famous and is prized by museums today. Tightly woven baskets ranging from horsehair miniatures to large plaques and sifter baskets continue to be produced by the Pueblos. Woolen rugs, intricately loomed by Navajo weavers, are truly a thing of beauty today and continue to demand high prices. Zuni inlay, Hopi overlay and Navajo nugget jewelry bring buyers from all over the world to Santa Fe and New Mexico.

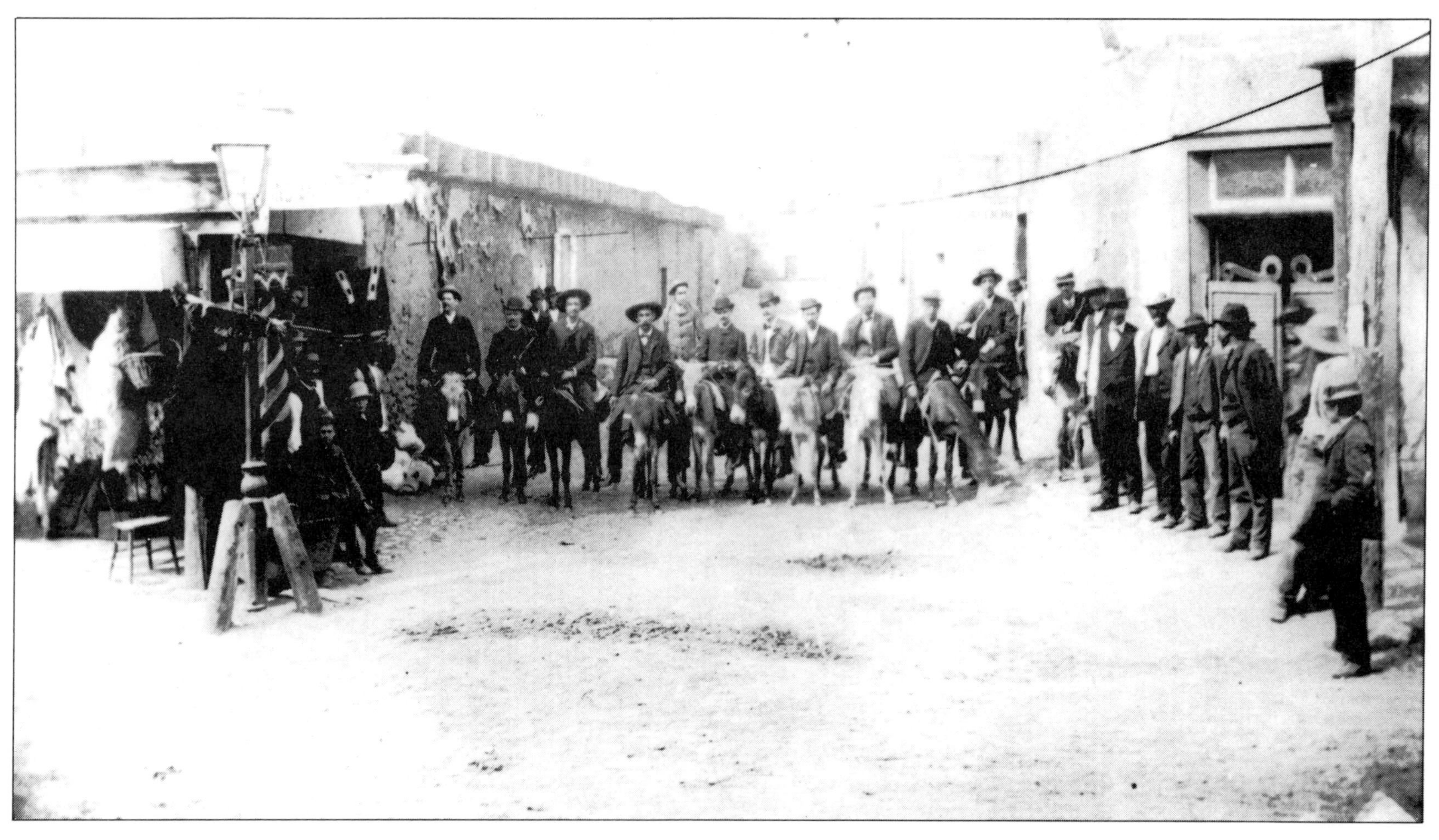

THEN — BURRO ALLEY, ca. 1880-1885

Just what inspired this collection of dudes to pose for a picture on burros in Burro Alley no one knows. Perhaps it was a convention of salesmen out for a good time. Burro Alley was the heart of the "good-time" district with its saloons, gambling dens and bawdyhouses. Jake Gold's Old Curiosity Shop is on the left-hand corner. Note the wooden planks flanking the streetlight. A later picture of Burro Alley shows the lamppost battered and beaten, proof of the rough and rowdy days of "Taos Lightning" (the local whiskey) and five-card stud.

SW7

NOW — BURRO ALLEY

The smell of burro dung, dust and gunpowder has long since vanished. The Alley remains with a few shops along it, connecting West Palace Avenue and lower San Francisco Street. Gold's Old Curiosity Shop is now the corner of the Lensic Theater building. Doña Tules Barcello's monte parlor, which was in the vicinity of Burro Alley and Palace Avenue, is now the location of the Santa Fe County Courthouse.

Chapel, Fort Marcy, ca. 1864-68

NORTHWEST

NW1

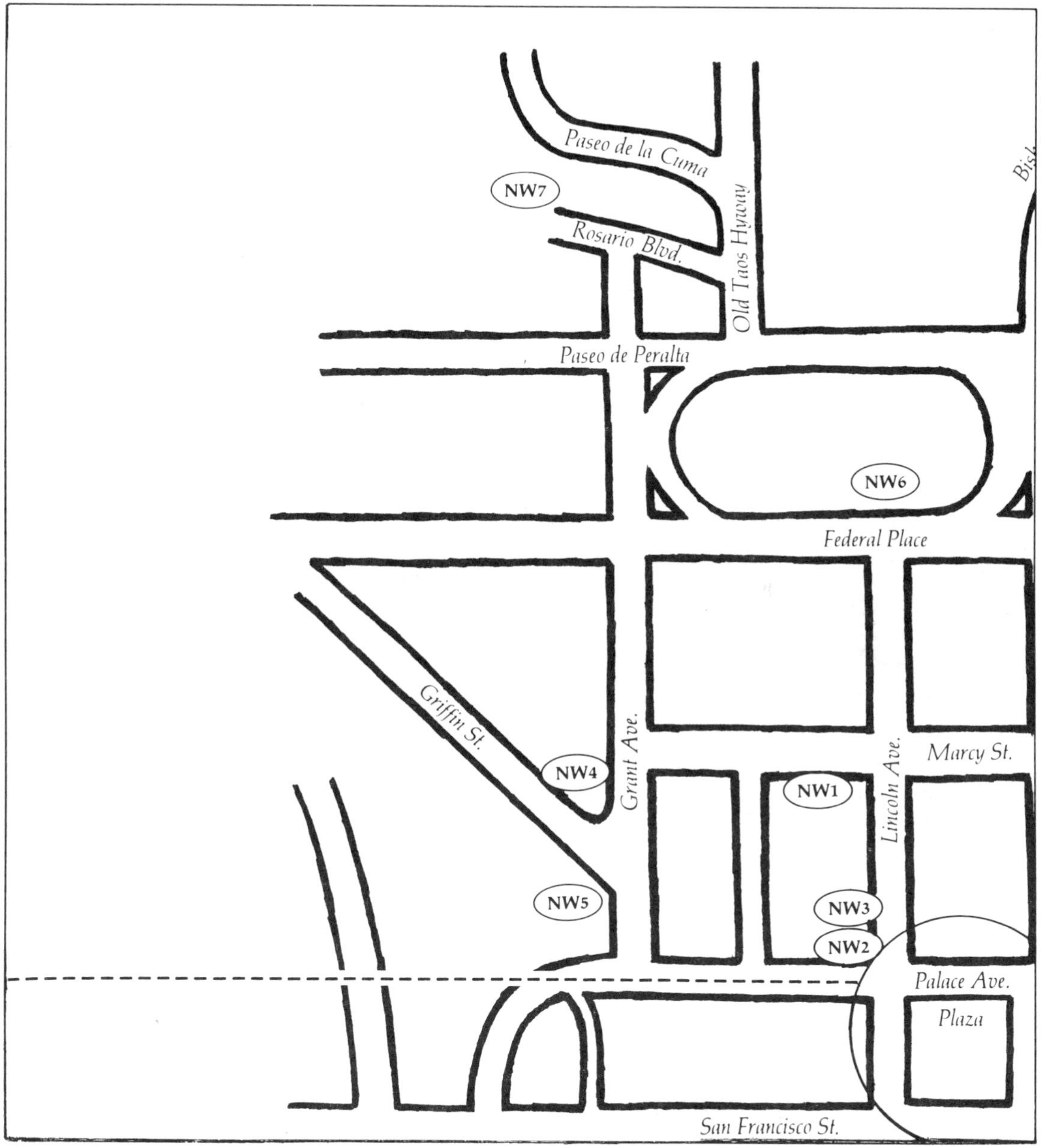

Paseo de la Cuma
NW7
Rosario Blvd.
Old Taos Hyway
Paseo de Peralta
NW6
Federal Place
Griffin St.
Grant Ave.
NW4
Lincoln Ave.
Marcy St.
NW1
NW5
NW3
NW2
Palace Ave.
Plaza
San Francisco St.

THEN — FORT MARCY HEADQUARTERS, ca. 1880, (inset ca. 1916-17)

When the U.S. Army, under General Stephen W. Kearny, took over Santa Fe in 1846 and declared New Mexico a U.S. territory, Kearny ordered construction of a fort on the hill north of the city, to be named Fort Marcy after William L. Marcy, Secretary of War. It was a star-shaped adobe structure, the first U.S. military post built in the Southwest but, ironically, it was never garrisoned, needed or used. Instead, the army utilized the barracks, corrals, vegetable gardens and existing buildings of the Spanish/Mexican presidio already in place north of the Plaza.

Fort Marcy Reservation was created in 1868 and the headquarters was constructed in 1870 in Territorial style according to a plan designed in Washington, D.C. The military reservation included 17 acres by the Executive Order of President Andrew Johnson in 1868. The reservation was abandoned by the Army in 1894 as unnecessary. The purchase of New Mexico had been secured from Mexico 40 years before and the lengthy Indian wars finally came to an end in 1886.

NW2

NOW — FINE ARTS MUSEUM

In 1916 the Fine Arts Museum, shown under construction, replaced the old Headquarters bulding. The Spanish-Pueblo styled structure was the first addition to the Museum of New Mexico, already housed in the Palace of the Governors. It incorporated authentic features from 300-year-old mission churches located at Laguna, Acoma, San Felipe, Cochiti and Pecos and was the beginning of the trend toward similar architecture, now termed Spanish-Pueblo Revival.

The Museum houses a wonderful permanent collection of Southwestern art including paintings, sculpture, drawings, prints and photographs. In addition, there are often special exhibits on loan from other museums.

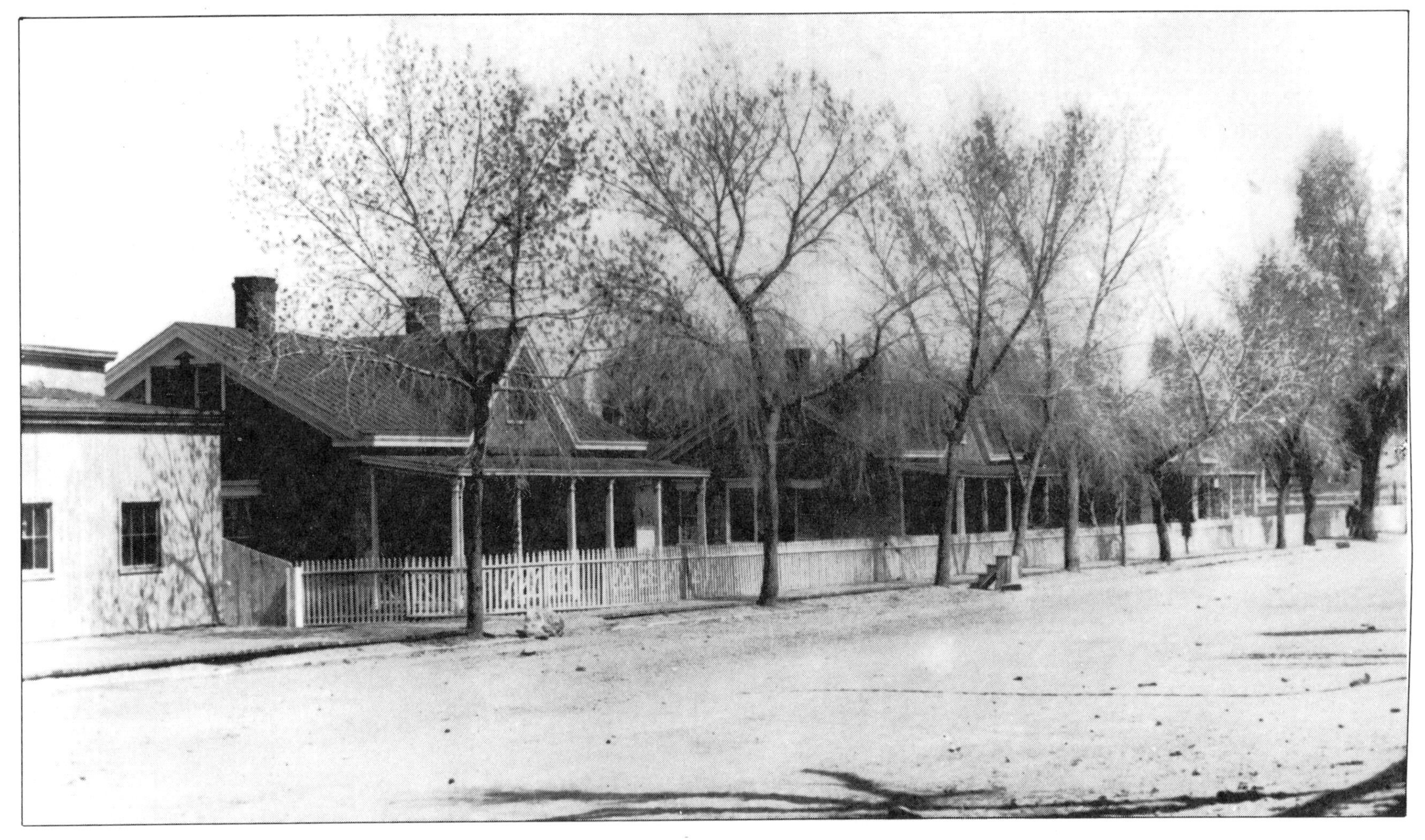

THEN — FT. MARCY OFFICERS' RESIDENCES
ca. 1880

With the creation of Fort Marcy Reservation in 1868, six adobe houses were constructed in the early 70s for officers' use on Grant and Lincoln Avenues. They were a modification of the U.S. Army's standard "Plan C," two-storied with a cross-gable roof.

After Fort Marcy was abandoned, the homes came under the jurisdiction of the Interior Department and the property was administered by the governor of New Mexico. They were used as rent-free residences by political leaders and other prominent citizens. John R. McFie, Associate Justice of the New Mexico Territorial Supreme Court, resided in the first home on the left.

NW3

NOW — FT. MARCY OFFICERS' RESIDENCE

Out of the six homes built, only two remain. The second one, located at 135 Grant Avenue, is just through the block. The McFie home changed hands several times before it was purchased by attorney Frank Springer in 1916. Springer was a member of the board of regents of the Museum of New Mexico and president of the managing board of the School of American Research. He ordered the home remodeled into the Spanish-Pueblo style in order to serve as a residence for Dr. Edgar Lee Hewett, director of both the School and Museum. In 1917 Springer gave the property to the School and it was used as their headquarters from 1959 to 1972. It is now owned by the Museum of New Mexico.

The other two homes came into private ownership during the 1900s. One was purchased by Dr. Joseph Foster and the third was eventually purchased in 1906 by territorial governor Herbert J. Hagerman. Hagerman sold it to Charles E. Doll, who lived there until 1948 when both his home and that of Dr. Foster were purchased by Sears, Roebuck & Co. The homes were razed and the present building was constructed.

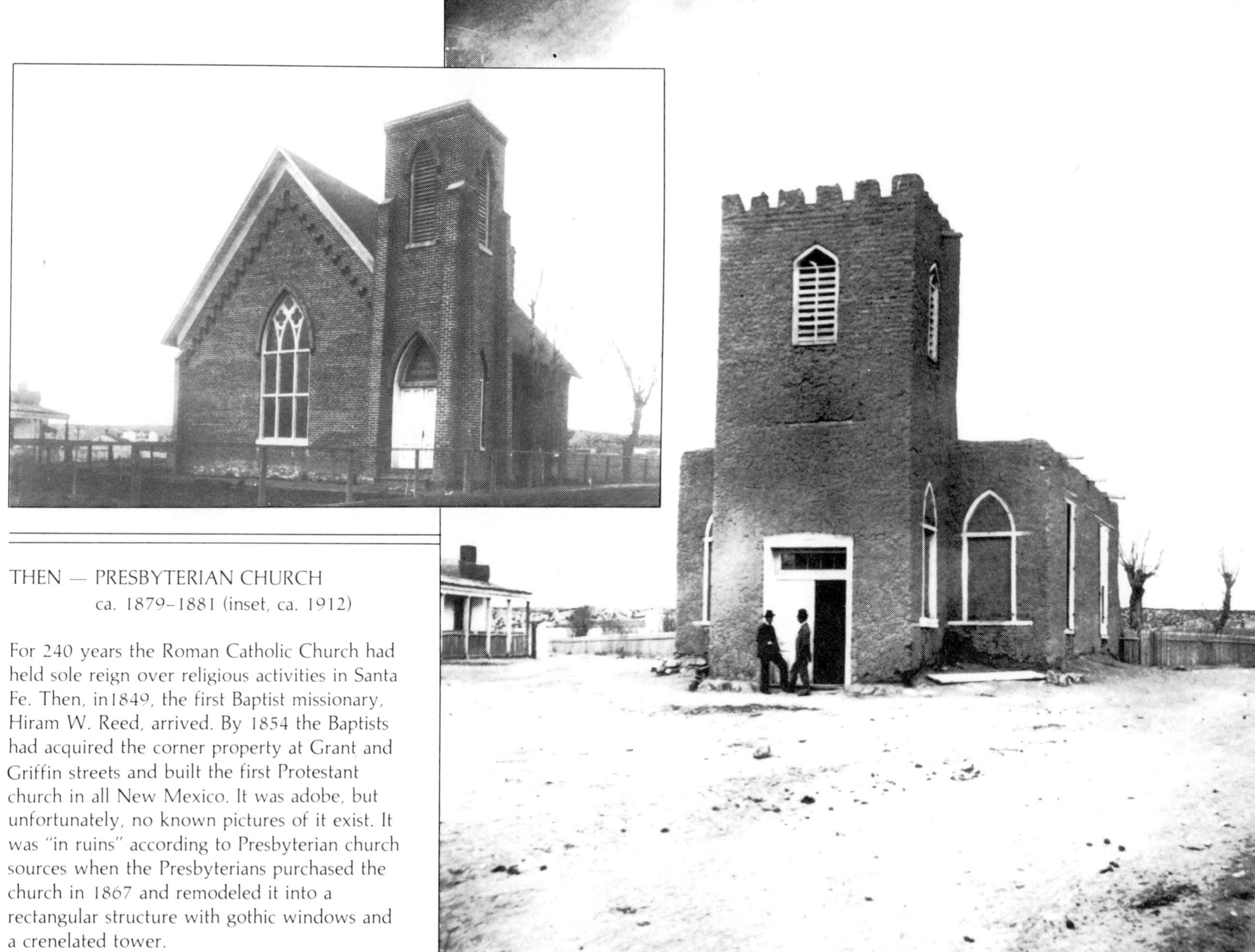

THEN — PRESBYTERIAN CHURCH
ca. 1879–1881 (inset, ca. 1912)

For 240 years the Roman Catholic Church had held sole reign over religious activities in Santa Fe. Then, in1849, the first Baptist missionary, Hiram W. Reed, arrived. By 1854 the Baptists had acquired the corner property at Grant and Griffin streets and built the first Protestant church in all New Mexico. It was adobe, but unfortunately, no known pictures of it exist. It was "in ruins" according to Presbyterian church sources when the Presbyterians purchased the church in 1867 and remodeled it into a rectangular structure with gothic windows and a crenelated tower.

NW4

NOW — PRESBYTERIAN CHURCH

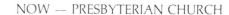

In 1912 the adobe building was completely remodeled into the Gothic Revival brick structure shown left. The most recent renovation – a particularly lovely Spanish-Pueblo design in the mission style — occurred in 1939 under the direction of John Gaw Meem. Although its architectural style has changed several times, the Presbyterian church has occupied this same site since 1867, giving it the distinction of being the oldest Protestant church in New Mexico.

Santa Fe, still a relatively small city, now includes a wide spectrum of religions, both Christian and non-Christian. Evolution amid tradition, diversity amid uniformity are some of the elements which make Santa Fe the cosmopolitan city it is today.

THEN — PINCKNEY TULLY HOUSE
ca. 1910

It was always an attractive house, styled in Territorial design and had the distinction of having the first bay window in Santa Fe. It was adobe construction, built in 1851 by Pinckney R. Tully on property donated to him by his father-in-law James Conklin. The Tullys moved after only three years and the property went through a long succession of owners including the publisher of Santa Fe's first English newspaper, Oliver P. Hovey, Padre Gallegos, the ex-priest, the first U.S. surveyor-general for New Mexico, a secretary of the Territory, and attorney general (who added the tenth room with the bay window), a bank president and a chief justice of the New Mexico Supreme Court.

NW5

NOW — 136 GRANT AVENUE

The house had many alterations made to the interior but the exterior has remained true to its original construction with the exception of the bay window. The house was purchased by the Historic Santa Fe Foundation in 1974 after it was threatened with demolition. The exterior was restored to the 1890s style, which included "stenciling" or "tatooing" the surface to look like brick. Upon restoration, a small portion of the original "brick" was saved and is exposed under the south portal.

THEN — FEDERAL BUILDING, ca. 1890-91
(inset ca. 1878-84)

Another in the series of contradictions in New Mexico's long history was the original capitol building, often identified as the "Federal Building" in old photographs. Money was appropriated by Congress in 1850 and again in 1854, but when the funds were spent, the building was only one and one-half stories high. It remained in that condition until 1883, the year of the Tertio-Millennial celebration. L. Bradford Prince (later governor of the territory) and Arthur Boyle, an agent for British land investment interests, were among the socially prominent promoters of the six-weeks-long event intended to attract visitors and new businesses, via the railroad, to Santa Fe. Humorously, the organizers miscalculated the founding of Santa Fe by 59 years: the 333-year celebration should have been held in 1942. In any event, the half-finished building was temporarily put into service to house the Indian participants in the celebration by adding a floor and roof. A race track was laid out encircling the building for horse, mule and burro races. Indians did tribal dances and graciously assisted with a reenactment of the battle with the forces of Conquistador Francisco Vasquez de Coronado.

NW6

NOW — U.S. COURTHOUSE

The building was finally completed in 1889, together with its circular stone wall, but by then a new capitol building had been constructed and it was no longer needed for that purpose. Instead, the Court of Private Land Claims and the U.S. Land Office took it over.

In 1885 a simple stone monument was erected in honor of the military scout, guide, officer and Indian agent, Kit Carson, at the south entrance to the courthouse.

The U.S. District Court and other federal agencies use the building today. Constructed of native stone, it is still an outstanding example of Greek Revival architecture and one of the few buildings in the West of its age and design untouched by renovation.

THEN — HAYT-WIENTGE MANSION,
ca. 1890

In 1882, on a hill overlooking the city, Walter V. Hayt built a Victorian "mansion." Hayt was a New York merchant who operated a stationery and notions store on San Francisco Street. The home was small but beautifully constructed of hand-molded, fired adobe brick.

Comparing the surrounding traditional flat-roofed adobe homes with this Victorian "mansion" emphasizes the diverse directions architecture was taking near the end of the 19th century.

NW7

NOW — 620 PASEO DE LA CUMA

Hayt sold the home in 1888 to Mrs. Frederick W. Wientge of New Jersey, whose husband was a well-known jewelry designer. They added a brick room to the northeast corner in 1899 for Mr. Wientge's use as a workshop. Members of the Wientge family occupied the house until 1972. The house has had various owners and uses from that time. Of all the historic homes in Santa Fe, it is one of only two retaining a mansard roof. The home, still a landmark today, continues in striking contrast to its "Santa Fe style" condominium neighbors.

Bibliography

Alexander, Ruth Laughlin. *The Wind Leaves No Shadow.* Enl. ed., Caldwell, ID: Caxton, 1956.

Baldwin, Brewster, and Kottlowski, Frank E. *Santa Fe. Scenic Trips to the Geologic Past, No. 1.* Socorro, NM: State Bureau of Mines and Mineral Resources, 1968.

Bradford, Richard. *Red Sky At Morning.* New York: Pocket Books, 1969.

Bullock, Alice. *Discover Santa Fe.* Santa Fe: L. Lavender, 1973.

______________. *Loretto and the Miraculous Staircase.* Santa Fe: Sunstone Press, 1978.

Cartwright, Jean and John. *Enjoy Santa Fe More.* Rev. ed. Santa Fe: New Mexico Publishing Co., 1983.

Cather, Willa. *Death Comes for the Archbishop.* New York: Vintage, 1971.

Chauvenet, Beatrice. *Hewett and Friends, A Biography of Santa Fe's Vibrant Era.* Santa Fe: Museum of New Mexico Press, 1983.

Chavez, Fray Angelico. *La Conquistadora: The Autobiography of an Ancient Statue.* Rev. ed. Santa Fe: Sunstone Press, 1983.

Coke, Van Deren. *Taos & Santa Fe, The Artists Environment, 1882-1942.* Albuquerque: University of New Mexico, 1963.

Gibson, Arrell Morgan. *The Santa Fe and The Taos Colonies: Age of the Muses, 1900-1942.* Norman: University of Oklahoma Press, 1983.

Hertzog, Peter. *La Fonda: The Inn of Santa Fe.* Santa Fe: Press of the Territorian, 1962.

Hillerman, Anne. *Children's Guide to Santa Fe.* Santa Fe: Sunstone Press, 1984.

Historic Santa Fe Foundation. *Old Santa Fe Today.* 3rd ed. Albuquerque: University of New Mexico Press, 1982.

Horgan, Paul. *The Centuries of Santa Fe.* Santa Fe: Wm. Gannon, 1976.

______________. *Lamy of Santa Fe.* New York: Farrar, Straus and Giroux, 1975.

Jamison, Bill. *Santa Fe, An Intimate View.* Santa Fe: Milagro Press, 1982.

Jordan, Louann. *How To See La Villa Real de Santa Fe and Enjoy Your Vacation.* Santa Fe: Press of the Territorian, 1972.

LaFarge, Oliver. *Man With The Calabash Pipe.* New York: Houghton-Mifflin, 1966.

______________. *Santa Fe, The Autobiography of a Southwestern Town.* Norman: University of Oklahoma Press, 1959.

League of Women Voters, Santa Fe County. *This is Santa Fe, A Citizens' Handbook.* Santa Fe: 1974.

Muth, Marcia. *Is It Safe To Drink The Water? A Guide to Santa Fe.* Rev. and enl. ed. Santa Fe: Sunstone Press, 1983.

Nusbaum, Rosemary. *The City Different & The Palace.* Santa Fe: Sunstone Press, 1978.

Ortega, Pedro Ribera. *Christmas In Old Santa Fe.* 2nd ed. Santa Fe: Sunstone Press, 1982.

__________. *La Conquistadora: America's Oldest Madonna.* Rev., bilingual (Eng./Span.) ed. Santa Fe: Sunstone Press, 1984.

Pillsbury, Dorothy. *Adobe Doorways.* Santa Fe: Lightning Tree, 1983.

__________. *No High Adobe.* Santa Fe: Lightning Tree, 1983.

__________. *Roots In Adobe.* Santa Fe: Lightning Tree, 1983.

__________. *Star Over Adobe.* Santa Fe: Lightning Tree, 1983.

Porter, C. Fayne. *Santa Fe In Haiku.* Santa Fe: Ortiz Printing Shop, 1970.

Reeve, Kay Aiken. *Santa Fe and Taos, 1898-1942: An American Cultural Center.* El Paso: Texas Western Press, University of Texas at El Paso, 1982.

Robertson, Edna, and Nestor, Sarah. *Artists of the Canyons and Caminos: Santa Fe, The Early Years.* Salt Lake City: Gibbs M. Smith, 1982.

Santa Fean, A Monthly Magazine. 1972–

Scott, Eleanor. *The First Twenty Years of the Santa Fe Opera.* Santa Fe: Sunstone Press, 1976.

Sherman, John. *Santa Fe, A Pictorial History.* Norfolk, VA: Donning, 1983.

Shiskin, J.K. *An Early History of the Museum of New Mexico Fine Arts Building.* Santa Fe: Museum of New Mexico Press, 1968.

__________. *The Palace of the Governors.* Santa Fe: Museum of New Mexico, 1972.

Simmons, Marc. *Yesterday in Santa Fe: Episodes in a Turbulent History.* Cerrillos, NM: San Marcos Press, 1969.

Snow, Cordelia Thomas. *A Brief History of the Palace of the Governors and a Preliminary Report on the 1974 Excavation.* [Santa Fe: 1974].

Thomas, Justine, and King, David. *Santa Fe, The City Different.* Santa Fe: Sunstone Press, 1979.

Thompson, Waite, and Gottlieb, Richard. *Santa Fe Guide.* Rev. ed. Santa Fe: Sunstone Press, 1984.

Weigle, Marta, and Fiore, Kyle. *Santa Fe and Taos, The Writer's Era, 1916-1941.* Santa Fe: Ancient City Press, 1982.

Wilson, Christopher Montgomery. *The Santa Fe, New Mexico Plaza: An Architectural and Cultural History, 1610-1921.* Thesis (M.A.) University of New Mexico, 1981. Albuquerque, 1981.

NOTE: Although some of these titles may be out-of-print, they can usually be found in libraries or ordered from book dealers who specialize in secondhand or out-of-print Southwestern material.

Photo Index

The following photographs, listed with their file numbers, their photographers, and in order of their appearance in the book, are courtesy of the MUSEUM OF NEW MEXICO:

All other photographs courtesy JOHN SWENSON.

General Index